The Benefits Of Altruism

Increase Your Desire to Serve Others

Abijah MANGA

Identifiers: ISBN: 978-1-958851-04-3 (e-book) / ISBN: 978-1-958851-03-6 (paperback) / ISBN: 978-1-958851-05-0 (Hardback) Title: The Benefits Of Altruism / Description: First Edition.

Cover design by: Derek Creative

MIB Consulting LLC Control Number: 20221856975309
www.mabij.net / fondationmabij.com / lovinghomecare.net

Printed in the United States of America

MIB Consulting LLC
22 Bissette Drive, Colchester VT 05446
(802) 829-0338
info@mabij.net

Contents

Introduction

Have you ever encountered someone who was truly worried about your well-being? Is this person considerate, courteous, and frequently concerned with the needs of others rather than their own? Some of the people who display these traits are said to as self-sacrificing. They feel good about themselves when they satisfy others. But on the other hand, they frequently feel selfish, guilty, and self-centered when focusing on their needs. Individuals with this profile are extraordinary in certain ways, and they may be extremely motivating in others. But, on the other hand, being a self-sacrificer might come at a high price.[1]

We see that self-sacrificers frequently pursue caring activities or pick careers that require them to serve other people's needs for considerable sections of the day. It makes the self-sacrificer happy when their efforts have a beneficial impact on the lives of others. One of the primary issues with this profile is that the self-sacrificer might be exploited, which can lead to resentment, rage, and even hate. Anger is frequently turned inward, which can lead to anxiety or depression. Think about that for a moment. If you have a self-sacrificer in your life, they are the folks who appear to be the happiest when they are helping others and potentially even themselves! However, suppose their attention is overly dependent on helping others. In that case, individuals in their life may grow acclimated to how they function and may be taken advantage of,

---

[1] "21 Selfish People Traits And What To Learn From Them (2022)." https://www.coaching-online.org/selfish-people/.

mistreated, or both. We frequently hear about family members or acquaintances supported (emotionally and financially) by the self-sacrificer. It will come to a head, like any other relationship, if the balance of giving and taking is off.

One of the most difficult ideas for the self-sacrificer to understand is assertiveness. That is, being able to declare what they require and why they require it with confidence. Putting their needs forward causes them to worry, and they struggle with what they need and desire against what they should be "perceived" to need and want. We frequently encounter these behaviors in persons with additional characteristics such as high trait anxiety, "people pleasers," perfectionists, and the concerned. It appears to be correlated with anxiety, which might be related to the fear of being perceived as selfish, being concerned about putting their needs first, or anxieties of being rejected while not helping. Often, the self-sacrificer wants to be recognized and acknowledged for their efforts.[23]

At Headway, we feel that the self-profile sacrificer's components should be acknowledged and promoted, such as their desire to bring enjoyment to others and make the world a better place to live. However, we must assist the self-sacrificer in developing assertiveness so that they are not taken advantage of, preventing them from getting resentful. Self-sacrificers can benefit greatly from psychological counseling. Their early experiences are frequently related to a great desire to please and serve others. With a little

---

[2] "10 Great Ways to Deal with Selfish People - Lifehack."
https://www.lifehack.org/articles/communication/10-great-ways-deal-with-selfish-people.html.

[3] "4 Ways to Deal With Selfish People | Psychology Today."
https://www.psychologytoday.com/us/blog/the-couch/201403/4-ways-deal-selfish-people.

guidance, the self-sacrificer may learn to be more aggressive and prioritize their own needs. The self-sacrificer will be better equipped to assist others and follow their passions if they learn to be more forceful.

CHAPTER-1

How To Sacrifice Your Time To Help Others

What Is Altruism?

Altruism is the selfless care for others—doing things just because you want to assist, rather than because you feel forced to do so due to duty, loyalty, or religious reasons. It entails acting out of concern for the welfare of others. In certain circumstances, these acts of selflessness cause people to put themselves in danger to aid others. Such activities are frequently carried out unselfishly and with no expectation of return. Other types of reciprocal altruism entail doing things to benefit others with the hope that they would do the same for you.

Altruism is defined as acting to enhance the benefit of others, even at the danger or expense of our own. Contrary to conventional assumption, individuals are innately self-interested, as revealed by a recent study: Even non-human primates show compassion intuitively, according to study. Children's altruism is based on concern for the welfare of people in need. According to evolutionary experts, altruism has deep roots in human nature because assisting and cooperating boost our species' survival. Indeed, Darwin maintained that altruism, often known as "sympathy" or "benevolence," is a "vital component of social instincts." Recent neuroscience research has demonstrated that when people act altruistically, their brains engage in areas that convey pleasure and reward, comparable to when they consume chocolate (or have sex). Altruism is the act of helping someone else at the expense of oneself. It can involve everything from risking one's life to rescue others, donating money to charity, working at a soup kitchen, or just waiting a few seconds to hold the door open for a stranger. People frequently act altruistically when they witness others in difficult situations and feel empathy and want to help.[4]

Altruistic desires and actions contribute significantly to the glue that holds families and social groupings together, allowing them to cooperate and prosper. Intangible rewards like recognition, respect and financial assistance are commonplace for those who go above and beyond to serve others. Altruism and the reciprocation of nice actions ensure that all members of a close-knit community receive support when needed. Altruism is commonly defined as an activity

---

[4] "11 Habits Toxic Coworkers Have In Common To Watch Out For In ... - Bustle." https://www.bustle.com/articles/188879-11-habits-toxic-coworkers-have-in-common-to-watch-out-for-in-the-office.

that benefits others at the expense of the individual. However, different writers in evolutionary biology have understood the idea of altruism differently, resulting in disparate predictions regarding the evolution of altruistic behavior.

Furthermore, various views disagree on who benefits from the generosity and how the cost of altruism is calculated. We outline alternative interpretations' assumptions and explain how they connect using a basic trait-group framework. We properly believe that a careful investigation of the relationships between interpretations not only explains why various writers have reached divergent findings concerning altruism but also exposes the conditions likely to encourage altruism's development.

We all have strongly entrenched behavioral dispositions ranging from charity to egoism. The difficulty is figuring out how to be altruistic without sacrificing our self-interest. Put another way; we are inherently conflicted between helping others and benefitting ourselves. So, what's the best way to find a middle ground? First, we must define altruism and understand what motivates people to be altruistic. Altruistic conduct, in essence, emphasizes the benefit of others. But what is the source of our good intentions? Is charity always beneficial, or does it have drawbacks? Is it required for work? This section will discuss altruism's advantages and disadvantages, the psychology behind it, and how to cultivate it in yourself and others.[56]

---

[5] "Altruism Definition & Meaning - Merriam-Webster." https://www.merriam-webster.com/dictionary/altruism.

[6] "What Is Altruism? - Verywell Mind." https://www.verywellmind.com/what-is-altruism-2794828.

Examples Of Altruism

Everyday acts of kindness abound, from holding the door for strangers to donating money to those in need. News stories frequently highlight bigger acts of kindness, such as a guy diving into a freezing river to save a drowning stranger or a contributor who donates thousands of dollars to a local charity. Here are some examples of altruism:

- Doing something to aid someone else without expecting anything in return
- avoiding items that may provide personal benefits if they impose costs on others
- Despite personal expenditures or hazards, assisting someone
- Even in times of shortage, sharing resources is essential.
- Concern for the well-being of another

Types Of Altruism

Psychologists have discovered several forms of altruistic conduct. These are some examples:

1. **Genetic altruism:** As the name implies, this altruism entails performing selfless acts for close family members. For example, to care for the needs of family members, parents and other family members frequently engage in acts of sacrifice.

2. **Reciprocal altruism:** This altruism is founded on a reciprocal give-and-take interaction. It entails aiding

someone now in the hopes that they may be able to repay the favor later.

3. **Group-selected altruism** entails performing altruistic deeds for people depending on their connection with an organization. For example, people may devote their energies to assisting members of their social group or supporting social issues that benefit a specific group.

4. **Pure altruism:** This type, also known as moral altruism, entails assisting someone else even if it is hazardous and without remuneration. Internalized ideals and morals inspire it.

Altruism is a selfless activity that benefits others. It entails some type of goal-directed action that benefits someone else's well-being. If you're altruistic, you act out of goodwill and a genuine desire to serve others, not out of obligation. Your drive derives from real care for the well-being of others, even if it means sacrificing your own. Altruism may be classified into several forms, ranging from genetic altruism to group-selected altruism and a few others. Each sort of altruism has its motivation. Each category will be discussed in the next section, along with some examples of altruism. Reciprocal altruism entails reciprocity, which means you help someone because they may be able to help you one day. Possibly you do a favor for a communications team member in the hopes that they would suggest you for a position when one opens up. The difficulty with this form of generosity is that it can lead to disappointment if they do not reciprocate.[78]

Nepotistic altruism, often known as genetic altruism, is conduct that benefits family members. In parent-child interactions, this form of altruism is frequent. Parents give up their time, money, and energy for their children's happiness. As a result, genetic generosity is inextricably tied to the human survival instinct. Pure altruism, often known as moral altruism, is the most selfless type of altruism. It entails assisting people without expecting anything in return, especially if there is a high danger involved. Group-selected altruism is compassion that is motivated by group affinities. For example, you could prefer to aid close friends rather than strangers through a charity. Maybe you're involved in a cause close to your heart, like a campaign to raise money for a program dedicated to suicide prevention.

Explaining Altruistic Behavior

While we are familiar with benevolence, social psychologists are curious about why it occurs. What motivates these random acts of kindness? Some people are willing to jeopardize their own lives to aid a stranger. One facet of what is known as prosocial conduct is altruism. Prosocial conduct is any activity that benefits others, regardless of the motivation or how the provider benefits from the action. However, not all prosocial efforts may be described as wholly selfless. We may assist others for several reasons, including guilt, responsibility, duty, or monetary compensation. We don't know why

[7] "Altruism - Wikipedia." https://en.wikipedia.org/wiki/Altruism.
[8] "Altruism | Psychology Today." 19 Oct. 2012, https://www.psychologytoday.com/us/basics/altruism.

altruism occurs, but psychologists have proposed several theories. First, psychologists have long argued whether some people are just born with a natural propensity to help others, a notion that claims altruism is affected by genetics. Second, kin selection is an evolutionary hypothesis that claims that people are more willing to aid blood relations since doing so increases the likelihood of gene transmission to future generations, ensuring the maintenance of shared genes. Third, people are more willing to help if they are linked. Finally, prosocial characteristics like compassion, cooperation, and empathy may also have a genetic foundation.

Altruism activates the brain's reward centers. Neurobiologists have shown that when people act altruistically, their brain's pleasure regions become more active. Compassionate behaviors stimulate parts of the brain involved with the reward system. Compassionate deeds provide favorable sentiments, which perpetuate altruistic behavior. Interactions and relationships with people have a substantial influence on generous conduct, and socialization may have an impact on charitable activities in early childhood. According to one study, youngsters who witnessed basic reciprocal acts of generosity were considerably more likely to engage in altruistic behavior. Friendly but non-altruistic behaviors, on the other hand, did not produce the same consequences. Modeling altruistic deeds can help youngsters develop prosocial and compassionate behaviors.

Observing prosocial conduct appears to lead to helpful behavior in adulthood. The laws, customs, and expectations of society can all impact whether or not people participate in altruistic conduct. The reciprocity norm, for example, is a social expectation in which we feel obligated to help others if they have already helped us. For example, if a buddy borrowed you money for lunch a few weeks ago, you'll undoubtedly feel obligated to repay them when they ask for $100. They did something for you, and now you feel bound to reciprocate.

While the concept of altruism is doing good for others without expecting anything in return, cognitive motivations may not be visible. For example, we may assist others in alleviating our misery or because being good to others reinforces our perception of ourselves as kind people. Other cognitive explanations include the empathy-altruism hypothesis, which proposes that people are more inclined to participate in altruistic conduct when they feel empathy for the person in distress. As their feeling of empathy grows, children tend to become more altruistic. The negative-state relief concept proposes that charitable acts can assist reduce the bad sensations associated with witnessing someone else in misery. Seeing another person in suffering makes us unhappy, distressed, or uncomfortable, but assisting them alleviates these unpleasant sensations.[9][10]

Impact Of Altruism

While excessive generosity can have negative consequences, it is a beneficial force that can help you and others. Altruism has several advantages, including:

- **Better health:** Altruism has been shown to promote physical health in various ways. Volunteers had higher overall health,

---

[9] "Altruism Definition | What Is Altruism - Greater Good." https://greatergood.berkeley.edu/topic/altruism/definition.

[10] "Altruism Definition & Meaning - Merriam-Webster." https://www.merriam-webster.com/dictionary/altruism.

and helpful actions are associated with a much-reduced death rate.

- **Better mental well-being:** Doing nice for others can help you feel better about yourself and the world. According to research, people report higher enjoyment after doing good for others.

- **Better romantic relationships:** Being kind and compassionate may also improve your connection with your spouse since kindness is one of the most significant attributes people of all cultures look for in a love partner.

In addition to these advantages, altruism may strengthen social ties and relationships, eventually contributing to better health and wellness.

Fostering Altruistic Behavior

While some people are born with altruistic tendencies, there are things you can do to encourage helpful behaviors in yourself and others. These are some examples: Consider inspirational persons who perform selfless activities. Seeing how others are actively working to better the lives of individuals and communities might motivate you to behave altruistically in your own life. Instead of alienating yourself from others, exercise empathy by making connections and putting a human face on the problems you observe. Consider how you would feel in that circumstance and what you might do to help make a difference. Find methods to do random acts of kindness for others regularly. Seek around you for those who may want assistance or look for opportunities to volunteer in your community. Make dinner for someone in need, assist a friend with a task, donate blood at a blood drive, or volunteer for a local charity.

Potential Pitfalls

Altruism can have various costs and challenges, such as - It can occasionally entail risk. People may perform selfless deeds that put them at risk. People may sometimes disregard their physical, social, or financial requirements to care for others. While acts of charity are often performed with noble intentions, they do not always result in favorable consequences. It may encourage people to concentrate their energies on one cause while ignoring others. Caring for and assisting others can be emotionally draining for those who work in the helping professions. In a more severe case, a person who adopts animals altruistically may develop an animal hoarding problem, eventually unable to shelter or care for the animals they have taken in. Despite these possible issues, altruism is widely seen as a beneficial influence in the world and a talent worth cultivating.

Although compassion and empathy are not the same, compassionate empathy motivates people to aid others with whom they have social connections. This link fosters emotional and cognitive empathy. Empathy implies you comprehend someone's predicament, grasp their point of view, and can imagine yourself in their shoes. This comprehension naturally compels you to assist them. Altruism has the potential to stimulate pleasure areas in the brain. This indicates that completing an unselfish act can make you happy. Altruistic practices, according to scientists, can help alleviate physical suffering. According to research, altruistic parents can inspire their children to be altruistic.

Another example is helping others. When someone demonstrates selflessness by assisting you, you may feel obligated to assist them. For example, if a neighbor offers to keep your children while you work late, you may feel compelled to do the same for them when they require it.

Is it thus our nature to assist others? According to Hamilton's kin selection hypothesis, benevolence is intrinsic in humans and animals. Some charitable behaviors are naturally reactive. When we perceive those in need, we are naturally inclined to assist them. However, we learn generosity via our surroundings, upbringing, and societal standards.

Difference Between Altruism And Selfishness

Selfishness is solely concerned with own gain, whereas 'genuine altruism' is the pinnacle of selflessness. This is because it is done without the expectation of return and, in some situations, can put the giver at significant risk — for example, if you are a volunteer fireman. 'Reciprocal altruism,' on the other hand, might be called selfish since the giver expects the kindness to be repaid one day. On the surface, altruism and selfishness appear to be opposed. Altruism is a desire to assist others without concern for personal gain. Selfishness, on the other side, is the drive to please oneself while indulging one's desires. The selfish individual reaps their benefits without consideration for others. Selfishness is a normal human drive to defend oneself and behave in one's own best interests. In times of need or societal instability, selfish individuals will want to safeguard their interests and the interests of their immediate family. The feelings associated with this are entirely self-centered. The generous individual gives of their time, talents, and material things without expecting anything in return. It may look that way, yet there is a significant emotional reward to contributing. The generous individual derives enormous self-satisfying emotional gain from unselfish giving, on the other hand, casts a different perspective on this activity. It turns altruism into a selfish act of giving to fulfill personal sensations of doing good. These two terms appear to be opposed. A closer look into the psychology of their meaning finds an element of selfishness in altruism, making them more similar than one may believe. The question is whether they are real opposites or whether the benevolent character of altruism allows for some type of selfish feel-good feeling to be present.[11][12]

Both of these behaviors are accompanied by strong sentiments of emotion. Selfishness appears to be characterized by undesirable feelings such as avarice and self-absorption. Altruism appears to be viewed through the lens of positive emotions such as empathy and compassion. However, they share a sense of dread, albeit in different ways. Selfish individuals are afraid of having to give away everything they own.

In contrast, generous people are afraid of not being kind enough and failing to satisfy their goal of serving others. Both of these behaviors are accompanied by strong sentiments of emotion. Selfishness appears to be characterized by undesirable feelings such as avarice and self-absorption. Altruism appears to be viewed through the lens of positive emotions such as empathy and compassion. However, they share a sense of dread, albeit in different ways. Selfish individuals are afraid of having to give away everything

---

[11] "What Is Altruism? - Verywell Mind." https://www.verywellmind.com/what-is-altruism-2794828.

[12] "Altruism - Wikipedia." https://en.wikipedia.org/wiki/Altruism.

they own. In contrast, generous people are afraid of not being kind enough and failing to satisfy their goal of serving others.

Altruism is widely accepted in society. People who give unconditionally are considered nice, kind, caring, and giving. On the other hand, selfish people are perceived as greedy and inconsiderate about others. The only time selfishness is acceptable is when it is an act of self-preservation for the person and their immediate family.

True selflessness should not be accompanied by loud clapping and physical acclaim. Altruism can manifest itself in the form of physically assisting others, which is part of the act of giving. When a person purposefully steals something belonging to another and retains it for himself, selfishness becomes physical. Our psychological desires are driven by both selfishness and generosity. Our decision to display these various attitudes to life might be strongly tied to our upbringing and surroundings. Growing up, a youngster goes through several stages of growth and development. Stable parenting and setting excellent examples bring out the many aspects of this innate personality feature, which can be selfish or selfless.[13][14]

What Is Healthy Selfishness?

Selfishness has a negative reputation. Is it, however, all that bad? Healthy selfishness is defined as valuing one's wants and emotional well-being over the welfare of others. A typical example may be

---

[13] "Altruism | Psychology Today." 19 Oct. 2012,
https://www.psychologytoday.com/us/basics/altruism.
[14] "Altruism Definition | What Is Altruism - Greater Good."
https://greatergood.berkeley.edu/topic/altruism/definition.

during a plane's in-flight safety instructions. Securing your oxygen mask before assisting others with theirs is a good type of selfishness. There are two basic forms of altruism that most of us exhibit. We might be too self-absorbed and wrapped up in our troubles to care about the needs of others, or we can have a people-pleasing propensity and go out of our way to put others first, even if it involves self-sacrifice. Healthy selfishness can assist us in striking that balance. A good dose of selfishness may be found in your everyday activities, whether eating breakfast or napping when you're exhausted. Being healthily selfish means being aware of your physical, mental, and emotional well-being and meeting your own needs. The irony is that it is not at all selfish. Taking care of your own needs is, in reality, an act of generosity to both yourself and others. This is because when you show up for yourself, you can show up for others who rely on you, whether your children or your most important customer.

Is It Worth Sacrificing Yourself For Others?

Have you ever given up anything important to you to help another? It is commonly stated that self-sacrifice for love necessitates leaving something behind. However, love should never be associated with loss but rather with gain. We admire those willing to give up what is vital to them for something that has higher worth for them at the time. For example, giving up their jobs to raise their children, leaving their nation and family for a new spouse, preceding a nice existence to conduct humanitarian work... There are several instances.

Above all, it entails deciding between two options. The last one is picked because it looks to be more relevant, essential, or even fulfilling at the moment. From a psychological standpoint, we know that self-sacrifice has always been an element of being human. It does not, however, necessarily result in emotions of well-being or happiness. In reality, while it's possible to perceive significance and purpose in your acts at any given time, there will always be a period when you feel a feeling of loss, lack, and even regret.

When you hear of somebody sacrificing themselves for the sake of others, it piques your interest. That's because, as a general rule, you hold a gloomy perspective of other humans. You tend to think of them as more prone to selfishness than altruism, to own interest rather than compassion. The truth, however, is rather different. In truth, our survival as a species is due to our sense of belonging to a community and the attendant sentiments of collaboration. Dr. Mary McGrath of Yale University performed research that found that the type of teamwork we had in our evolutionary history implies that, in some ways, we still believe that giving something up for someone makes sense and is valuable. But, in truth, we've always sacrificed ourselves for the sake of others. Parents do it for the sake of their children. We make sacrifices for our jobs and the people we care about. Some people have martyr complexes and spend their entire lives sacrificing themselves. Others, on the other hand, will not even take the first step toward such gestures of aid and obedience. For decades, the area of psychology has been researching self-sacrifice. It's curious about what dimensions, situations, and individuals we as humans are willing to make sacrifices for. Because not all circumstances lend themselves to taking this step. As a result, not everyone in your life merits you to make sacrifices for them.

A sacrifice should never turn you into a victim or leave you dangling mid-air. For example, you do not have to give up your life for someone, but you may give up something particular to obtain something more valuable. For example, you may leave your city or even your nation for someone you love in the hope of bringing about brighter times. Sacrificing oneself for others makes sense if it enhances your reality or gives you more significance in your life. The latter is significant since it is all too often for this sacrifice to be forced rather than chosen. These men and women feel compelled to save others and make significant sacrifices for the greater good. The Cambridge Institute of Brain and Cognition Sciences did research that developed an intriguing idea. According to the study, characters who need to overthrow and sacrifice for others are motivated by nearly painful and selfish altruism. In reality, they hope to alleviate their pain through their deeds. For example, if they are unhappy or feel horrible about themselves for a certain reason, they opt to give up everything. This is a therapeutic experience for them. As you can see, self-sacrifice takes many forms. The extremes, however, would be those imposed by society and those inflicted as a penance by oneself.[15][16]

Sacrificing Yourself For Others

In life, you must risk and sometimes even take tremendous leaps of faith without knowing what will happen. Everyone has sacrificed for something or someone at some point in their lives. It occasionally goes wrong. For example, suppose you jumped without a parachute, and your reckless action backfired. However, that was what you

---

[15] "Altruism (Stanford Encyclopedia of Philosophy)." 25 Aug. 2016, https://plato.stanford.edu/entries/altruism/.

[16] "What Is Altruism? Examples and Types of Altruistic Behavior." 24 May. 2022, https://psychcentral.com/health/altruism-examples.

thought at the time because you were sure of it and lacked the experience you now have. As a result, it wasn't a mistake; it was just another stage of life from which you learned. Making sacrifices is something that you do regularly. In reality, you carry them out more often for persons you care about. You sacrifice for your partner, children, family, and other people who are important to you.

Furthermore, you are sometimes rewarded for your actions. Finally, attempt to ponder and find more balance in your life regarding who and why you perform these tiny or huge acts of sacrifice. Remember that individuals are motivated by altruism rather than selfishness. This dimension will always bother you and force you to confront it. [17]

Leaders who change the world usually make enormous personal sacrifices. According to Paul Hargreaves, "their journey frequently begins with a purpose to do the right thing and a sense of feeling powerful enough to do this; through this, they acquire compassion for others, which means they leave an incredible legacy." Many incredible stories of self-sacrifice have emerged after the 9/11 catastrophe, but none more so than those of Richard Rescorla, a British-American Vietnam War veteran. On September 11, 2001, he worked as a security director at Morgan Stanley. When he learned of the initial jet hit on the North Tower of the World Trade Center, he calmly urged about 2,700 Morgan Stanley workers to leave the South Tower, despite an earlier notification ordering them to remain at their workstations. He made certain that everyone for whom he was responsible had exited the building before beginning his exit. When the building fell, he was still inside. Rescorla was

---

[17] "What Is Altruism in Psychology? 8 Inspiring Examples." 03 Sept. 2020, https://positivepsychology.com/altruism/.

proclaimed dead three weeks later, but his corpse was never located. This is one of many incredible stories of self-sacrificial behavior under difficult situations, including a person laying down their lives in the ultimate act of self-sacrifice.

The Importance Of Helping Others

In our technologically advanced environment, we may go a whole day without seeing or talking to another person. We can work, get food, and do almost everything else from home, thanks to digital devices and the Internet. You can spend days without interacting with anything other than your touch screen, mouse, or keyboard. And while technology isn't necessarily harmful in and of itself, it does make it easier for individuals to be isolated. But it is not the world we want to live in. There are many wonderful aspects of our contemporary world, but the people who inhabit it should be at the top of the list. Taking an authentic interest in your family, friends, neighbors, and even strangers is one of the most gratifying decisions you can make for yourself and those you choose to serve. Consider the last time you assisted someone, whether it was holding the door open for a classmate or raking the leaves of an elderly neighbor. How did you feel while performing it and afterward? We're guessing you felt happier and more optimistic about life. This is because assisting others is the quickest way to feel joy.

However, serving does more than only make your heart happy. Studies have demonstrated that serving has mental and physical health advantages such as decreasing blood pressure and increasing longevity. Put the needs of others above your own, and you'll strengthen your relationships. It connects you to the individual you're aiding; If that person is someone you know, it strengthens your relationship with them. It also improves the lives of others. Taking the effort to bring a cup of soup to a friend who is ill is a small gesture that may make a big difference in their recovery. The possibility of that individual paying it forward is possibly the finest benefit of service. If you help someone, they are more likely to help someone else that day. Your one act of kindness might set off a chain reaction.

There is some evidence that helping others might cause physiological changes in the brain associated with happiness. This increased sense of well-being may be the consequence of being more physically active due to volunteering, or it may be the effect of it making us more socially engaged. Making new acquaintances and connecting with our community can be facilitated by assisting others. For instance, volunteering at a food bank can also help alleviate feelings of loneliness and isolation among the elderly. According to research, volunteering improves a person's overall feeling of purpose and identity. This is because assisting others may make you feel pleased, happy, and empowered. Donating your time and resources to needy people is an excellent way to gain perspective and increase self-esteem.

According to one study, people are more inclined to undertake acts of charity after witnessing someone else do so. This influence has the potential to spread across the community, encouraging hundreds of others to make a difference. Volunteering regularly can increase your abilities to handle stress and sickness while also enhancing your feeling of life happiness. This might be because volunteering reduces loneliness and improves our social life. You were helping others teaches you how to assist yourself. If you've had a difficult event or have a case of the blues, the "activism cure" is a terrific way to feel more like yourself. Volunteers have been reported to have greater self-esteem and general happiness. The advantages of volunteering are also dependent on your constancy. By doing voluntary work regularly, you will gain confidence. When you serve others, you emit positive energy that might rub off on your peers and boost your friendships. Being a positive influence in your friend's life can help you form a lasting friendship. Making a big difference in the lives of others may help you transform your view and attitude. According to experts, committing acts of kindness improves your mood and makes you happier and more positive.[18][19]

Humans are social beings. When we are isolated, we suffer; when we are part of a group, we thrive. Altruism occurs when we give a helping hand to people of our community, even if it costs us something. Helping others does not always come cheap, but the benefits are not always evident. Humans begin to exhibit generosity at an early age. This means that it is not something we are socialized for but rather something built into our brains. According to scientists, helping others ensures the survival of the human species. When contemplating evolution, this appears to be contradictory. If generosity is in our genes, shouldn't it be confined to others who share our DNA? That is not the case, as individuals frequently assist strangers, even when it is dangerous. Many different sorts of researchers and scientists are involved in this long-standing question.

---

[18] "Altruism: Meaning, Examples, Types, Benefits, and More." https://mantracare.org/therapy/what-is/altruism/.
[19] "Altruism - Ethics Unwrapped." https://ethicsunwrapped.utexas.edu/glossary/altruism.

Researchers investigating benevolence go beyond humans to the rest of the animal kingdom. They discovered that animals occasionally aid each other even when there is no obvious advantage to themselves. In one experiment, monkeys were given food, but when they consumed it, it shocked another animal. The monkeys started refusing food. A bottlenose dolphin guided two beached whales to safety in 2008. In many circumstances, animal altruism is not selfless since there is some advantage to the donor, but in other cases, that conclusion is erroneous. What is going on is still being investigated.

Brain chemistry supports the notion that compassion is "hardwired" in humans. In a study published in Science, researchers paid participants $100 and placed them in an fMRI machine. They were then offered the option of donating their money to a food bank. Donations were voluntary or involuntary, allowing scientists to distinguish between donating voluntarily and being compelled to donate. More dopamine in the brain was linked with processing unexpected rewards when subjects contributed voluntarily. This activation might explain why people continue to contribute even though it costs them anything.

You feel better about yourself when you help someone else. The individual you assisted feels happy as a result of your actions. This gives you a great sense of belonging and connection. People are more likely to feel safe and happy in societies that respect compassion and selflessness. The inverse is also true. There is less social connectedness in societies where no one supports each other. The good sensations you experience from helping others influence how you view yourself. According to research, when individuals contribute, especially to someone they don't know, it boosts their self-esteem. Giving money, working with an organization, or performing random acts of kindness are all ways to contribute. A variety of variables contribute to healthy health. Helping others may also play a role. A group of persons with high blood pressure was given money by a study team from the University of British Columbia. Each participant received $100 to spend on themselves, with the other half directed to give it to a friend or family member as a gift. People who spent money on others had much lower blood pressure than those who spent money on themselves a few weeks later.[2021]

Helping others is not just beneficial to your health; it may also help you live longer. One 2003 research looked at a group of elderly persons. Some of them provided social assistance while others received it—giving social assistance after five years made a person more likely to be alive after the research period. This was true even when researchers adjusted for physical and mental health, marital status, etc. Many people do not associate the job with compassion and generosity. Work may be competitive, which is often incompatible with assisting others. However, studies demonstrate that helpful environments are associated with more sales, better goods, and higher productivity. Employees need to assist one another. When people are driven by personal gain, they are less likely to assist. Offering assistance before it is sought is likewise frowned upon in the job.

---

[20] "What Is Altruism (and Is It Important at Work)? - BetterUp." 19 Oct. 2021, https://www.betterup.com/blog/altruism.

[21] "What Is Altruism, and Why Is It Important? | Teachers College, Columbia ...." 15 Dec. 2011, https://www.tc.columbia.edu/articles/2011/december/what-is-altruism-and-why-is-it-important/.

Being helpful, as we all know, promotes social bonds. As a result, relationships become stronger and more rewarding. Kindness, empathy, and helpfulness contribute to pleasure and fulfillment in love relationships. When people approach their relationships with a giving perspective, all connections, including friends and family, benefit. Humans have long sought to understand the purpose of life. According to research, it may be related to helping others. Researchers questioned 400 participants in a pilot study published in The Journal of Positive Psychology on how frequently they engaged in philanthropic activities and how meaningful their lives felt. Participants who reported higher levels of compassion perceived more significance in their lives. Why? It might be due to the link between altruism and improved connections and social connection, which research consistently demonstrates is crucial to a person's sense of purpose.

CHAPTER 2

Be Generous

What Is Generosity?

Generosity is defined as being kind, unselfish, and kind to others. Despite being an act done to promote the well-being of others, generosity paradoxically increases our well-being. Giving is thus an excellent method to boost your mental health and well-being. Not sure how to proceed? Continue reading to learn how to be a more charitable person. Generosity is beneficial to our mental health and well-being because when we give to someone we care about, we increase the likelihood that they will give to us, which increases our likelihood of giving to them, and so on. As a result, pleasure, social connection, and trust-related areas of our brain light up, making us feel warm and gooey inside. It turns out that developing positive thinking skills is an essential step in making the most of our generosity. Why? Because good feelings like appreciation, pleasure, or amazement increase our likelihood of giving. The more content we are when we contribute, the more inclined we are to give to others in the future. And in general, the more appreciative we are, the more we appreciate the experience of seeing others benefit from our contributions. So, if we're having trouble becoming more charitable, we can benefit from practicing positive thinking.

Fortunately for us, generosity is our default setting. However, we might unintentionally overcome our natural impulses to provide it by focusing too much on the "thinking" aspects of our brains. Our innate tendency to be kind may lead us to find reasons to withhold our generosity, such as the desire to purchase something for ourselves or fear of running out. But if our objective is happiness (for ourselves or others), we make a tremendous error. Giving to others makes us happy than spending money on ourselves. So, strive to overcome your worry of not having enough, which might prevent you from being more generous. How can we become more generous if we are willing to attempt (either for our own or for the enjoyment of others)? We might offer gifts on holidays, to recognize achievements, or simply because we felt like it (my favorite time to give a gift). We may also perform random acts of kindness, such as sending a thoughtful note to a coworker, emailing a family member to express gratitude for something they did, or purchasing lunch for a friend. Focus on donating in ways that positively influence someone else's life to make it even more fulfilling (not just your life). The more our belief that what we contribute will be worthwhile or beneficial to others, the better it feels. We genuinely want to know whether or not we are making a difference. So offer with thinking and meaning. It only makes us and the present receiver feel better.[22][23]

How To Be Generous

Being generous begins with treating each individual as though they have already realized the grandeur inside each of us. Giving something voluntarily and gladly without expecting anything in return is generosity, whether the money to a cause you believe in or time to a buddy in need. In essence, generosity is the genuine desire to improve the lives of others to make them simpler and more enjoyable. So, how can you foster generosity? Someone should be honored. Make a huge production of your friend's birthday the next time it comes around. Get a large cake, invite friends, and arrange a party to make the recipient feel cherished and special. Celebrate the birthdays of the people that matter most to you, even if you don't celebrate your own. You may find any reason to celebrate someone, from a birthday to a promotion, or just because you want to.

Be courteous to strangers. Even if it's simply saying hello to someone you've never met before, complimenting someone in line at the grocery store, or holding a door open for someone carrying groceries, taking the time to be kind to strangers is incredibly generous and simple. Taking the time to be courteous to strangers is even more generous if you're in a hurry. Give some of your time to a buddy. If a buddy is sad and lonely, you should be generous with your time and spend time with that individual. Plan a date with

---

[22] "The truth about altruism - Harvard Health." 05 Jan. 2016, https://www.health.harvard.edu/blog/the-truth-about-altruism-201601058929.
[23] "ALTRUISM | meaning in the Cambridge English Dictionary." https://dictionary.cambridge.org/dictionary/english/altruism.

that person, whether for a walk, a movie, or just a cup of tea and a chat. There should always be a time in your schedule for socializing with friends, no matter how busy you are.

Donate to a cause in which you believe. Donating money to a respected charity does not need much money. Even if you give $10 every month, you'll be doing good in the world and feeling good about yourself. You should give this amount as soon as you get your paycheck, rather than wait until the month's end to see how much money you have left. You'll be amazed how little you'll miss having this money. Even placing some spare coins in a tip jar might be considered nice. Volunteer. It's a great way to demonstrate your generosity by giving your time to others. Spend an hour or two a week working at a soup kitchen, tutoring adults or children, cleaning up a neighborhood park, or doing some other good in the world if you want to be kind. You may do things like volunteer in a bookshop or help with a charity fundraising effort. Find something that offers you significance while also allowing you to be more generous. Share your belongings. If you're among friends, share your food, clothing, vehicle, home, or anything else that means anything to you. It's not as significant if you're merely sharing something you don't care about. If you only have two exquisite chocolates left and offer one to a friend, that's more than giving your buddy one of a hundred candy bars you don't want. [2425]

Give something you adore. Your favorite sweater should be given to your younger sister. Give a copy of your favorite book to a buddy.

---

[24] "Altruism: Characteristics, Theories and Advantages." https://itspsychology.com/altruism/.
[25] "115 Synonyms & Antonyms of ALTRUISM - Merriam-Webster." https://www.merriam-webster.com/thesaurus/altruism.

Give a lovely journal to a friend and encourage her to begin composing poems. Giving something away that you don't care about isn't truly being generous since you're not making a sacrifice. Giving up something meaningful to you that you know will benefit others is the pinnacle of generosity. Compliment someone. Aim to provide at least five compliments every week – or even daily – and be liberal with your pleasant words. Look for a meaningful remark or even something as basic as "I adore your jewelry" or "Those are such amazing spectacles" while talking to someone. Even the tiniest praise may brighten someone's day if it's genuine.

Send thank-you notes. Don't just thank the person by email or text; make it personal by sending them an actual letter. This will demonstrate to the individual how much you care and that you have made an effort to let them know how much their assistance has meant to you. Sending thank-you notes will give you a more kind and giving frame of mind. Call a buddy who is struggling. If you can't make it in person, contact your buddy to check in, say hello, and demonstrate that you care. It doesn't matter if they're still hurting if you can spare just a few minutes to explain that you care about them and that you're being genuine and pleasant. Spending time on the phone attempting to cheer up someone in need is incredibly generous.

Please vacate your seat. You've had a hard day at work, but the elderly gentleman above you may be far more exhausted. And the individual doesn't even have to be older; you may simply stand up and offer your seat to someone else since you don't need it, and it will feel nice. Give a sizable tip. Leave a generous tip if you've received great service or came into contact with a person needing a lift. At the bottom of the check, write a thank you letter informing the person how much they have improved your day.

Make a good internet comment for someone. Leaving a kind, approving remark on a stranger's blog or a friend's Facebook or Instagram account might make the individual feel better and demonstrate that you care. It will also be incredibly generous of you! Please hold the door open for someone. You should never be too exhausted to hold the door for someone or take time out of your day to be kind and kind to someone around, no matter how busy, late, or sleepy you are. This simple gesture will make you, and the other feel better and realize there is always time to slow down and serve others. Donate your belongings. Don't just leave old sweaters or clothing in your closet for years. Check them out and give the items to a charity so that someone else can benefit from them. It won't take long to pick through them or drive them down to where they need to go, and just thinking about someone else finding a better use for your things will make you feel good.

Make someone happy. If you notice someone who needs to be cheered up, whether it's a stranger or a relative, take the time to make that person happy, whether it's by telling a goofy joke, smiling at them, or doing a kind favor for them. Making someone grin may change their day, and you'll be given for attempting to make someone happy. Give with all of your heart. To be generous, you must contribute out of a genuine desire to help, not to receive compensation. You should donate just because you want to, because you believe in something, and because you want to do good in the world. If you're merely donating to impress others or to ingratiate yourself with someone, you're not truly being generous.

You should be aware that giving will make you happier. Though you should not be giving only to meet your wants, you should be aware that those who are generous are known to be happier than those who are not: Giving makes people more empathetic toward others, fosters a better feeling of community, and promotes a positive self-image. While giving to others, you may also be generous to yourself. If you are happier, you will have a more positive attitude in life and more energy to do good in the world. The upward trend will continue.

Take note of everything that would make someone's life simpler. Whether you're communicating with your neighbors or best friend, look at the individual you're speaking with and consider how you may help that person. Perhaps your coworker is anxious and needs the care of her dog while she travels to see her ailing mother in another town. Perhaps your closest friend's automobile broke down, and she requires transportation to school. Perhaps your mother is overworked and doesn't understand how much assistance she requires until you provide it. When you talk to someone, start thinking about how you can assist them rather than how they can help you.

Thank God for what you have. Being appreciative may encourage giving because it makes you aware of all the wonderful things in your life. At the absolute least, write down at least five things you're thankful for each Sunday. Consider all the excellent things individuals have done for you and never forget to thank them, even if it was months ago. Being more appreciative will put you in a better frame of mind to be more charitable. If you can enjoy what you have, you'll be more inclined to share some wonderful things, allowing others to appreciate life. Remember to be generous to yourself. Volunteering, caring for others, and donating your time are wonderful ways to be kind. You should not lose sight of yourself in the process. Remember to listen to yourself and identify what you want and need, whether it's a wonderful lunch out or a warm bubble bath. If you entirely disregard yourself for the benefit of others, you are likely to burn out and have less to give. It is not selfish to care about your wants and happiness. There is a distinction between being selfish and caring just about oneself.[26][27]

Practical Tips For Practicing Generosity

Generous individuals are healthier, happier, and more satisfied with their lives. Giving others your money, time, expertise, or kindness are examples of methods to practice generosity. Whatever time you have, you can make a difference. Generosity is simply the act of being nice and kind to others. Although it is an act to help others, acting generously improves your well-being. According to research, generous individuals are physically healthier, have more empathy, have reduced rates of despair, and even live longer. We promote the sensation of being able to make a difference in the world by being charitable and actively addressing the needs of people around us. Generosity has also been shown to have a cascading impact. According to research released by the National Academy of Sciences, cooperative conduct (also known as generosity or kindness) spreads up to three degrees of separation. In other words, when one person acts generously, two more individuals are

---

[26] "30 Top Pros & Cons Of Altruism - E&C." https://environmental-conscience.com/altruism-pros-cons/.

[27] "Altruism definition, types and examples - Toolshero." 10 Feb. 2022, https://www.toolshero.com/sociology/altruism/.

motivated or persuaded to do the same. There are several methods to donate; how you practice, generosity will be determined by your circumstances. However, the more you practice generosity, the more you will shift from someone who does generous things to someone who is giving.

When we are grateful for and appreciate what we have, we are more willing to offer generously. And because the more we give, the happier and more appreciative we feel, it's a self-perpetuating loop. Positive Psychology has compiled a list of some of the most popular gratitude activities, including journaling, gratitude prompts, thank-you notes, and meditation. Sometimes we focus on what we don't have rather than what we do. The fear of not having enough might cause us to be less giving. When we feel plentiful, on the other hand — when we see the glass as half-full and believe we have what we need now and will be cared for in the future — we are more likely to contribute to others.

Recognizing the needs of others necessitates paying close attention and learning to read between the lines. This is frequently referred to as empathetic listening. It occurs when you can progress from taking in another person's literal words to understanding what is being said emotionally. It also entails learning to understand what another person needs, regardless of what you would desire if you were in their circumstances, rather than making assumptions about their needs based on your preferences. Generosity works both ways. Some people find it simpler to give than to receive. Accepting charity, for example, may make some individuals feel weak, undeserving, or less autonomous. When you deny or dismiss someone's generosity toward you, they lose the thrill of giving.

Accepting charity can also help you become more compassionate and aware of the needs of others.

According to psychology, giving individuals are happier, healthier, and more satisfied with their lives than those who do not contribute. And giving improves your mental health in many more ways since it may increase your happiness, connection to others, and sentiments of trust. From a spiritual standpoint, generosity reduces attachment when presented with a loving, unselfish aim. That's good for you since attachment to things, people, situations, and oneself may bring a lot of pain when things change, as they eventually do. Learning to let go is also vital for spiritual growth. And being kind now may help you feel more at ease when death occurs and forces you to let go of everything.[28][29]

Surprisingly, giving is as helpful to the giver as it is to the receiver. But only when you contribute selflessly to benefit others without expecting anything in return. If you expect acclaim, fame presents or favors in exchange, and you will be bitter and dissatisfied if they do not come... these sentiments occur, and the joy of giving fades. Therefore, it is critical to select gifts intelligently. Never provide something dangerous. For example, giving a bottle of liquor to an alcoholic would not be considered generous.

When Generosity Is Hard - Start Small

Maybe you're afraid about running out of supplies or wondering if you'll need anything in the future. You were perhaps giving away

---

[28] "Altruism - The Decision Lab." https://thedecisionlab.com/reference-guide/philosophy/altruism.

[29] "Altruism Magazine | Altru Health System." https://www.altru.org/about-us/altruism-magazine/.

something as basic as your favorite mug causes your heart to skip. And, of course, you don't want to share half your candy bar since you could get hungry! These doubts and worries might be firmly ingrained in your unconscious mind. Contributing might cause some people to constrict, so don't be too hard on yourself. Despite all the ravings about the power of charity on this site, donating will not boost your sense of well-being if it causes terror in your heart. So, how can you overcome your reluctance to give? The key is to begin small.

People in the Buddhist tradition practice giving mentally. When you walk into a magnificent store, for example, you gift the richness you observe to all living beings. When preparing to have a delectable supper, you extend the invitation to everybody. Don't dismiss this practice as fictitious. It's an effective technique for gradually shifting your automatic attitude from stinginess to generosity. Offer praises, open the door for someone, or send a text message to a buddy on a special occasion. Small acts of kindness are free and require little time, yet they may greatly impact someone else's day. They also help you get out of your mind, where you're probably thinking about yourself, your troubles, and your world, and into thinking about others - the first step toward selflessness. Keep your options open. Allow for the benefit of the doubt. Instead of looking for flaws, concentrate on the advantages. Thank you. Consider others.

Begin with simple presents like a small amount of money, a cheap object, or simply a piece of fruit. Donations are accepted in a contribution box at the end of the checkout line at my local health food shop. I like the one that advocates for a cat and dog sanctuary.

Those in the United States who shop on Amazon might want to look at Amazon Smile. When you do, Amazon will donate.05 percent of your qualified Amazon Smile purchases to your chosen charitable organization. It's precisely the same as Amazon in terms of prices, products, and services, with the bonus of donating a portion of Amazon's profits to charity. You're not donating money, but choosing your organisation requires time and effort; remember to go to the Amazon Smile page rather than the normal one when you're ready to buy.

Most importantly, it begins to restructure your mind to think about the needs of others rather than always thinking "me, me, me," as most of us do. I'm not sure what "little" would mean to you. So, spend a little time brainstorming ten simple ways you may offer that would not put you in a panic. Then choose one of those. Practice these techniques for a time until you see an inner shift from fear or hesitancy to greater openness and desire to offer more. You won't necessarily change overnight, but you'll have more opportunities to be more giving.[30][31]

Material Possessions

Have you seen the Netflix show, Marie Kondo? Marie Kondo is a world-renowned decluttering expert, in case you didn't know. Each episode depicts a journey from clutter to greater simplicity. The quantity of enormous trash bags of "things" that come out of each residence, often 50 or 60 or more, is problematic. People in wealthy

---

[30] "Generosity Definition & Meaning - Merriam-Webster." https://www.merriam-webster.com/dictionary/generosity.

[31] "What Is Generosity? (And How to Be a More Generous Person)." 04 Feb. 2019, https://www.psychologytoday.com/us/blog/click-here-happiness/201902/what-is-generosity-and-how-be-more-generous-person.

nations amass incredible amounts of possessions. They frequently require a storage facility in addition to their residence. It's time to start giving up your material stuff. You'll most likely feel relieved. However, you are not limited to contributing only your goods. You might buy food, clothes, books, or other necessities for needy friends or family members. Ideas:

- Instead of tossing usable goods into the garbage, which contributes to plastic and other pollution, give them to friends at a charity store. As a non-attachment practice, several great Buddhist teachers gave up all of their belongings twice or three times during their lives.

- When someone compliments you on your outfit, openly offer it to them. They may object, but you must insist that they have it.

- Make a book donation to a Little Free Library.

- Make a food donation to a food drive.

Money

Everyone like receiving money, don't they? Make someone's day by being very kind.

- Give a large tip.

- Buy a ticket for a buddy to go to the movies, the theatre, or comedy performance.

- Donate to a homeless individual.

- Put your spare coins in the store's donation cans.

- Donate to charity organizations, no matter how large or little.

- Pay for the automobile in front of you in the drive-through.

- I bought a drink from a kid's lemonade stand and left them an additional tip.

Your Time

Nobody seems to have spare time these days, so offering your time is a true gift.

- Offer to babysit for friends so they may go out for the evening.

- Become a mentor to a youngster or share your skills and experience with someone at work two requires assistance.

- Call a buddy going through a difficult period merely to listen and support them.

- Volunteer for a charitable organization.

Protection From Fear

Help individuals who are recuperating from a disaster such as a storm, flood, or lava eruption, or who live in danger every day, such as people living in war zones.

- Spend some time volunteering in a battered women's shelter, an animal shelter, or a homeless shelter.

- Adopt a child.

- Help out in the aftermath of a calamity.

Your Body

Not everyone will be able to donate organs, and you may lack the physical strength to serve as a house builder. But when we die, we all have to give up our bodies, which are frequently our most valued possessions. So, even if you can't contribute it in these ways, it's good to consider the transient nature of your body.

- At death, register as an organ donor.

- While you're still living, consider donating a kidney to someone in need.

- Donate your blood; there is a great demand for blood donors.

- Volunteer with organizations such as Habitat for Humanity, where you may utilize your physical abilities and strength to benefit others.

- Work in vocations that put your life in danger, such as police officers and firefighters.

- Work in vocations where you may use your life energy to serve others, such as charities, non-profits, or aid work.

- Assist your elderly neighbor with challenging, physically demanding duties.[32][33]

Spiritual Wisdom

Instead of preaching or evangelizing, share spiritual teachings or truths with those who are open to them. Spiritual teachings can liberate us from unneeded pain. They are, in that sense, one of the most valuable presents that can be given.

With any compassion practice, you begin where you are and progressively increase your ability. You may become frustrated and eventually give up if you try to accomplish too much quickly. You may become frustrated and eventually give up if you try to

---

[32] "What is Generosity? - University of Notre Dame."
https://generosityresearch.nd.edu/more-about-the-initiative/what-is-generosity/.

[33] "What Is Generosity? - The Spiritual Life." https://slife.org/what-is-generosity/.

accomplish too much quickly. So don't offer in ways that cause you so much pain that you wind up in bad condition. That will not benefit you or anybody else. Simultaneously, if you want generosity to be a tool for awakening and lessening attachment, you'll have to extend yourself a little. But, once again, you may begin modestly and gradually increase your capacity. For instance, instead of one dollar, donate two. Give a morning instead of an hour. Instead of gifting your least favorite mug, offer your fave. Stretching yourself in this way will allow you to connect with that part of yourself that is tough to let go of and eventually soften it.

However, proceed with caution. Maintain constant contact with your own experience. Pull back if you experience bitterness, regret, or tiredness. Pause if you believe what you're doing isn't beneficial. Always believe in yourself and your intuition. Don't just contribute because you "should." The goal is to increase your capacity to offer with enthusiasm. You may still feel apprehensive or fearful, but the overall experience is good. Most people will need to increase their ability to donate progressively. Generosity frequently necessitates breaking a life-long tendency of "me first." Rerouting deeply embedded neuronal networks in our brain takes time. That is not to argue that everyone is selfish; there is a lot of kindness in the world. However, if you examined your thoughts for the greater part of a day, you would probably discover that the major focus is on you and your happiness or those closest to you.

Generosity Is Powerful

Generosity is a wonderful approach to shifting your focus away from yourself and your problems. People frequently remark that assisting others helps them put their problems into perspective. When generosity is done without notions or a distinct feeling of "giving, gift, and recipient" in Buddhism, it becomes a metaphysical activity that brings you closer to spiritual enlightenment. What does this imply? You're not thinking, "Wow, I'm so fantastic to be delivering this." It's the most amazing gift I've ever received. They should enjoy it." You offer with an open heart, and if thoughts of it arise, you let them pass. You do not cling to them to make them larger, more real, and more substantial. But, even if you can't practice giving in this "ideal" way, do your best. Give generously, and you'll discover a whole new universe. And, as psychologists claim, you'll be happier, healthier, and more fulfilled as a result.

Ways To Become A More Generous Person

Like many young children, you may recall studying the virtues we should live by in primary school, the list of attributes considered morally good.' You may have noticed virtues like diligence, patience, compassion, humility, and charity on the list. We hear a lot about giving during this time of year. Generosity is the act of giving generously and abundantly. Because December is the "season of giving," there is no better time to consider some easy ways to be charitable this holiday season. So, why is generosity vital in life, you may be wondering? Many individuals have investigated the advantages of charity. And the good news is that there are many! Generous people are frequently happier, more contented, and satisfied with their life. There's something magical about how giving back to others helps you feel better about yourself. It not only makes individuals feel more secure but also makes them more productive when giving. Although the Christmas season is famed for its generosity, it is required all year! Another incredible reward of generous giving is the great influence you may have on the lives of others. Not only will you profit from your generosity, but you never know what impact you may have on someone else. These little gestures may make a big difference, whether sending a warm lunch to a new mom, contributing money to your local fire station, or volunteering at the elderly home down the street.

Few people dislike the concept of giving.

E is a species that enjoys assisting others and confronting needs when we perceive them. Unfortunately, relatively few individuals are satisfied with the degree of generosity in their life. Most individuals I know wish they could offer more. And while there might be a variety of reasons for this, sometimes the simplest option is the best. To that end, we can take a few easy measures to make giving a more purposeful part of our lives. If you've never given out money or time, this is a fantastic place to start (no matter your current economic situation). On the other hand, some of these easy actions might be helpful if your objective is merely to increase your giving.[34][35]

Consider the advantages of giving. Generous individuals are happier, healthier, and more content with their lives than those who do not contribute. As a result of our generous actions, we gain the confidence that we can positively impact our community and help shape it into a healthy one. Generosity is often seen as the opposite of selfishness, but calculating one's benefits is an essential first step. Accept thanks. Make a list of the things you are grateful for in your

---

[34] "What Is Generosity? - ChurchPlanting.com." 16 Jul. 2012, https://www.churchplanting.com/what-is-generosity/.

[35] "55 Synonyms & Antonyms of GENEROSITY - Merriam-Webster." https://www.merriam-webster.com/thesaurus/generosity.

life. Your list does not have to be extensive. It will not take long. It doesn't need to be a tangible list (in your head, it will be completely sufficient). Spend more time focusing on what you already have rather than what you don't. When you start thinking that way on purpose, you might be shocked at how good you already have it... and you'll be more likely to share your life with others.

Begin on a tiny scale. If you've never contributed money before, start with $1. Don't be embarrassed to offer even a dollar. You have nothing to worry about: dozens of charities online accept credit cards, and you'll never meet the folks who record your $1 payment. The goal of this exercise, of course, is not to submit a $1 tax deduction on your year-end tax return. The goal is to get going. Begin with $5, $10, or $20 if that is more comfortable for you. But, regardless of the cash number, begin with something little. You have the means... That small push might help you gain momentum in your life toward giving. First, give. Make your first spend from your next paycheck an act of generosity. We frequently wait to see how much money we have left before deciding how much we can give away. The issue is that most of the time, nothing is left over when we start spending. The practice of spending it all is far too established in our life.

Calculate how much money you'll save and then donate it to a certain charity or cause. Whatever you select, I recommend picking something exciting to give up - something one-of-a-kind that you'll remember. Setting a time limit for the experiment should make it entirely doable. For example, Courtney Carver saved $225 by giving up Starbucks in one month. Next, fund a cause that interests you. Several charities/causes require your assistance. And a few of them are connected to the things you find most fascinating. What are you most enthusiastic about? Is it the environment, poverty, or religion that is to blame? Perhaps it's global peace, kid nutrition, or animal rights. What about education, civil rights, and safe drinking water? Identify your existing passions, identify a devoted organization around that cause, and enthusiastically assist them in their efforts. In my case, it means I donate money and time to Essex CHIPS. It is a community-based organization that encourages youth to make healthy choices. Because I've always worked with kids, this group was a logical extension of my previous interests. Consequently, it was a no-brainer to back them.

Find someone in whom you have faith. If you discover that you are more readily driven and molded by the individuals in your life than by organizations/causes, capitalize on that propensity. Take special notes of the people you admire the most in your life. What organizations/causes are they most passionate about? Who do they back? What makes them so enthusiastic about it? And how can you participate with them? Spend time with folks who are in need. Making room in your life for people who truly need your assistance is one of the most effective antidotes to non-generosity. After all, it is only a simple step from knowing someone in need to assisting someone in need. Most homeless shelters eagerly welcome volunteers and have protocols to help you get started. And rubbing elbows with the destitute may forever influence your perception of them.[36][37]

Spend time with someone who is giving. When I got the guts to ask precise questions of the proper person, I had one of the most life-

---

[36] "What is Generosity?." https://generosity.us/What_is_Generosity_.html.

[37] "A Christian definition of generosity - ActiveChristianity." https://activechristianity.org/christian-definition-generosity.

changing talks about giving I've ever had. "Have you always been generous?" I recalled asking. And then there was more: "When did you become so generous?" How did it all begin? How do you pick where to put your money? "How would you advise someone just starting?" It was a life-changing experience. And the other guy paid for the lunch... strange. Live a more simple existence. Decide to own less on purpose. Living a minimalist lifestyle may not automatically make you a more charitable person, but it will give you the room to do so. You will spend less money at the department shop. You'll have more time and energy to assist others. And the intentionality that develops in your life will assist you in recognizing the need for giving. Minimalism has led to numerous beneficial changes in my life, the most significant being more charitable. Generosity is rarely accidental. Instead, it is a conscious decision we make in our life. However, it does not have to be as tough as many belief. Starting with the simplest steps is sometimes the greatest option.

CHAPTER-3

Love The Elderly And Children

Express Love To Seniors And The Elderly

If your senior or older loved one life in an assisted living facility, it might be difficult to communicate your respect and appreciation meaningfully. And, as the holidays approach, it's more crucial than ever to show your loved one how much you care. To properly convey your love to your senior and older family members, use these recommendations from Arizona Homestead. Making time to visit your older relatives may seem obvious, but it is one of the most effective ways to convey your affection. A phone call now and then is fine, but a personal visit goes above and beyond and allows you to spend quality time with your loved one. You'll generate great memories while also demonstrating your concern for your kin.

Many of our older people appreciate revisiting happy recollections. Bring your loved one a beautiful scrapbook or picture album filled with photographs from their favorite occasions, such as a wedding day, a grandchild's birthday, or previous holidays. Go over the images with them and discuss each one. Another excellent approach to demonstrating devotion is keeping your loved one comfortable. Cold, unwelcoming environments might lead to melancholy and gloomy feelings. Bring products that make your loved one's living place more comfortable or brighten their room with colorful decor. Blankets, toss pillows, slippers, and plush bathrobes are among examples. They'll be reminded of your thoughtful donation whenever they utilize one of these goods.

Now is the moment to look for your older loved one as they looked after you as a youngster? First, maintain vigilance on your loved one's health and physical condition. If you detect that something appears to be amiss, you may rectify it right immediately. Senior family members may keep problems to themselves out of fear of burdening their carers, so being proactive will keep them happy.

How To Care For The Elderly

Making time for someone, no matter how busy you are, is possibly the most valuable thing you can do for them. Being physically and emotionally present for your older loved ones is not only helpful for their health (socializing may substantially improve a senior's well-being), but the act itself conveys a message that goes without saying: you care about them and are there for them. Unfortunately, many elderly persons choose not to express their concerns because they do not want to burden those who care for them any longer. If you suspect something is wrong, try to keep a close eye on your senior loved one. Bring up topics you believe are upsetting them and gently persuade them to tell you what's on their mind, but don't force them. Instead, simply inform them that you will be available to listen when they are ready to discuss it.[38][39]

All older individuals need is someone to listen to them relate their stories. If you aren't close to your senior loved ones, this is your time to get to know them better. Inquire about their childhood experiences and compare them to your own. Inquire about the aspects of their lives that they would alter. Don't forget to keep them informed on what's going on in your life! Exclusion may be painful, and we can all recall the agony of being on the outside looking in. Whenever there is an event, whether a tiny get-together or a large family reunion, make sure your senior loved ones are aware of it and join them if they are willing. Being near others is beneficial to them, especially if those individuals are dear to their hearts.

If you are concerned that an older family or loved one is having difficulty caring for oneself, it may be time to intervene and give assistance. Take the time to examine your loved one's requirements before you begin assisting them. They may require assistance with their medical needs or additional aid with their daily activities. If you cannot care for them alone, seek local alternatives such as assisted living facilities or in-home care services. Caring for others may be demanding, so make time for yourself!

---

[38] "Generosity: Anyone Can Learn to Be Generous - WebMD." https://www.webmd.com/balance/features/how-to-be-more-generous.
[39] "What is generosity? - Quora." 29 Apr. 2017, https://www.quora.com/What-is-generosity.

Providing Home Care

Assess your relatives' requirements in collaboration with them. Before offering care for an older person, you must determine what type of care will be most beneficial to them. Depending on their general health and ability to accomplish day-to-day duties, individuals may require anything from occasional assistance to continuous care. Talk to them, observe them, and collaborate with their healthcare providers to evaluate their requirements. For example, consider whether your loved one has trouble performing simple tasks like eating, moving about their house, getting dressed, or maintaining their hygiene. If this is the case, they may require home care from you or a professional caregiver. On the other hand, if they can still perform the majority of their fundamental daily activities without assistance, you may just need to give occasional assistance. You may, for example, volunteer to come over once a week to assist with errands or household duties.

Maintain as much involvement in their care decisions as possible. If your loved one believes that other people make all of their decisions for them, they may be more reluctant to take the assistance. Include them in all talks and choices concerning their care to make them feel more autonomous and in charge of their circumstances. Communicate with them freely and honestly, and get their feedback and ideas on any possibilities you are contemplating. For example, you may remark, "Dad, it appears that you're having difficulty keeping up with the chores these days. Do you think it would be useful for me to come in and help out every few days?" Actively listen to what they say about their needs or how they feel about the care alternatives you are considering. If they have any worries, listen to them carefully without dismissing or downplaying them.

Install home security measures. As a caregiver, you may help your loved one by making their home environment more accessible and safe, whether they are living alone, with you, or getting live-in care. Consult a doctor, an elder care professional, or a physical or occupational therapist about the types of adjustments that might be most beneficial to your loved one. They may, for example, require:

- Installed grab bars or handrails in restrooms, hallways, and other living areas
- Elevated toilet seats or shower seats
- Stair climbers or ramps
- Slip-resistant surfaces on stairs, floors, and showers
- Better lighting in low-light regions of the house, Anti-scalding devices in showers and sinks

Assist your loved one in remaining active. According to the Centers for Disease Control and Prevention, older adults should engage in 150 minutes of moderate activity per week. Encourage your loved ones to include moderate levels of physical exercise into their everyday lives to help keep them healthy and happy. Ask their doctor or physical therapist for advice on how much exercise to perform. A person with osteoarthritis, for example, might need to stick to low-impact activities like swimming, stationary cycling, or gentle yoga. Those unable to exercise on their own might nevertheless reap the benefits of regular exercise. For example, older persons can benefit from passive range of motion (ROM) activities. These exercises entail moving the individual's limbs to help loosen up their joints.

Request that a doctor or physical therapist demonstrates how to perform these exercises appropriately. Look for interesting hobbies you can do together, such as nature excursions or gardening.

Maintain your involvement in their medical treatment. Most older persons suffer from a range of age-related ailments and health issues. To ensure your loved one receives the best treatment, speak with them and their health care staff to become acquainted with their specific challenges. Keep a watch out for any new or worsening symptoms, and ensure they get medical assistance if their health changes. Familiarize yourself with any drugs they take so you are aware of potential interactions or negative effects. If they have difficulties remembering to take their meds, consider utilizing a pill sorter or contacting them regularly to remind them. Keep an eye out for typical warning symptoms of a health concern, such as amnesia or disorientation, falling or lack of coordination, weight loss or changes in appetite, or changes in mood or behavior. Emotional issues are very widespread among the elderly. [40]

Encourage them to interact with others. Spending time with friends keeps older persons physically, emotionally, and psychologically healthier than those who do not. Encourage your loved one to socialize as often as possible, even if it's only calling a friend. If they don't have a large social network, you may offer classes or other activities where they can meet new people, such as dances or book club meetings. Spending time with grandkids benefits many elderly folks. If you have children caring for an aging parent, consider

---

[40] "What Is Generosity? (And How to Be a More Generous Person)."
https://www.psychologytoday.com/au/blog/click-here-happiness/201902/what-is-generosity-and-how-be-more-generous-person.

asking them to babysit or do other pleasant things with the children, such as playing board games or reading stories.

Offer to assist with errands and tasks. Day-to-day duties such as cooking, cleaning, and food shopping can become more difficult to handle as individuals age. Discuss with your loved one what you can do to assist them in meeting these requirements. You could, for example, sit down with them once a week to make a shopping list, then go to the store and acquire what they require. If they have difficulty driving, offer to drive them to medical appointments, the grocery, or other locations they must regularly visit.

Discuss their money with them. Several expenses and financial issues are involved with aging, ranging from coping with medical bills to financing the price of home safety enhancements. If your older relative is retired, they may want extra financial assistance to pay their expenditures. Discuss their financial resources and devise a strategy to assist them if necessary. For example, if they want to stay at home but can't pay their existing rent or mortgage, you may talk about assisting them in finding a smaller apartment or condo that works within their budget. They could also be eligible for government assistance programs to help pay for things like heating bills or prescription drugs.

Taking Care Of An Elderly Person In A Hospital

Inquire with the hospital personnel about their care. Having an older loved one in the hospital may be frightening and distressing. However, you'll feel more at ease and better able to assist them if you understand their disease and treatment alternatives. Make a list of questions for their medical staff, such as:

- How long will they have to stay at the hospital?

- What are their therapy options for their illness?

- The pros and cons of this therapy are as follows:

- What steps are you taking to alleviate their pain and discomfort?

- What will the healing time be like?

Prepare to answer questions as well. Depending on their state, your older loved one may find it difficult to answer critical questions about their symptoms, health history, or drugs they are now taking. Discuss your loved one's treatment preferences with them. Engaging your elderly loved one as much as possible in major medical decisions is essential. If their condition permits it, discuss therapy alternatives with them. If not, attempt to follow their desires as best you can. For example, if you know they wish to avoid surgery, inquire about less invasive treatment choices with their doctor. Talk to your loved ones while they are healthy so that you know what to do if they have to be hospitalized.

If their needs are not being satisfied, they should be advocated for. If your older loved one is unwell or has communication difficulties, they may struggle to speak for themselves. If you believe they are not receiving enough care, don't be hesitant to stand up for them. Be aggressive while asking questions or notifying their care staff if they want assistance. For instance, you may need to:

- Ascertain that they receive their meds on schedule.

- Follow up on medical test findings.

- Speak with various care team members to ensure everyone is on the same page regarding their treatment plan.

Bring them whatever items they may require. Pack a backpack with whatever your loved one could need from home to keep them comfortable in the hospital. Make sure to include things like:

- Clothing that is warm and comfy, such as a few loose-fitting sweaters and soft sweatpants
- Slippers or socks with non-slip soles
- Toiletries and personal care products, such as a hairbrush, comb, toothbrush, glasses case, or dentures
- A nice and cozy cushion
- a list of their prescriptions
- Items of entertainment, such as beloved books, periodicals, or DVDs
- A framed image, a vase of flowers, or their favorite bathrobe are all nice touches.

They are regularly visited. Stop by as often as possible to keep your loved ones from feeling alone and ensure they receive the required attention. Try to be there when you know they may be lonely or upset, such as at mealtimes or when they undergo testing or medical procedures. Invite additional family members and friends to join you. This will not only make your loved one feel supported and cared for, but it will also relieve some of your stress.

Take care of the necessary documents. A hospital stay is usually fraught with red tape. Health care directives may be available to you and your loved ones if it is possible to get them. If your loved one is unable to sign permission documents or other hospital documentation, you may be required to do so. In addition, keep hold of any important paperwork connected to your loved one's hospital stay, such as bills, care, discharge instructions, and benefit explanation statements.

Create a hospital discharge strategy. Before your loved one leaves the hospital, speak with their care team about the type of care they will require in the future. Ensure you have information like - Dosage and timing instructions for any drugs they must take. You may need to know any unique home care procedures, such as changing wound dressings, caring for feeding tubes or catheters, or securely transferring your loved one about the house. Call these numbers if you have any queries or concerns regarding their status following discharge. Details about what to expect throughout the recuperation time.[41][42]

Finding Elder Care Resources

Request a referral from their doctor for a home healthcare provider. If you find that your loved one requires in-home medical care, their doctor may be able to refer you to a reliable service. They may also be able to prescribe particular in-home treatments (such as physical therapy or nursing), making insurance coverage for this sort of care simpler to obtain. You can also call your loved one's insurance company or your local health and human services agency to learn about local providers and how to handle related costs. If your relative needs assistance with everyday chores but does not require round-the-clock medical care, consider hiring an in-home care provider to assist them with house cleaning, cooking, dressing, and

---

[41] "Generosity vs. Giving. What Does It Mean to Be Generous?." https://www.mindfulschools.org/personal-practice/what-does-it-mean-to-be-generous/.

[42] "Generosity | SkillsYouNeed." https://www.skillsyouneed.com/ps/generosity.html.

bathing. You might find this helpful if you don't have the time or resources to help your loved one throughout the day.

If home care is not an option, look into nursing facilities. Living at one's own or a relative's house is not always practicable or inexpensive for the elderly. If you believe your loved one is unable to live independently and you are unable to give the necessary home care, look into nursing homes or other residential care choices in your region. People with medical concerns may benefit from residing in a nursing home with nurses and physicians on staff. Alternatively, an assisted living facility may be a wonderful alternative if your loved one needs assistance with everyday tasks but does not require daily nursing care. If you reside in the United States, you may search LeadingAge's member directory for quality elder care facilities and services in your region. When selecting a facility, chat to the staff and the residents to get a feel of the services offered and whether the facility will fit the requirements of your loved one.

Look for financial aid options in your region. If you are experiencing difficulty affording the costs of care for a loved one, you may be eligible for assistance. Depending on their requirements, you may be able to obtain funds to cover expenditures such as medical bills, housing costs, utilities, continuing education tuition, or food costs. Look for advantages in your region by searching online. Look for programs that offer older people food and other amenities. In addition to financial assistance, various programs and services are available to assist seniors with other needs. Your community, for example, may provide resources like free meals delivered to your loved one's home, aid with home repairs or home safety modifications, or free or low-cost legal services for seniors. Your local government website could include information about resources and services for the elderly in your region. Try searching for "resources for elders around me." If you require emotional support and assistance, join a support group. Caring for an aging relative can be difficult.

Dealing With Challenges

Be prepared to face opposition from your loved one. Many older people desire to be as self-sufficient as possible and may resent your efforts to care for them or link them with eldercare services. If this occurs, try to be patient and understanding. Take the time to communicate your worries with your loved ones courteously and open-mindedly, and do your best to accommodate their choices. Sit down with them when you are both calm and comfortable and freely discuss their requirements. If you have the backing of the rest of your family, it may be simpler to persuade your relative that they require further assistance. It may also be beneficial to get advice from their doctor. Try recommending a trial run once you've developed a careful approach. If your loved one understands that the arrangement isn't fixed in stone and may be modified if it isn't working for them, they may be more inclined to accept your care.

If they are having difficulty communicating, get help from their doctor. Many elderly persons have difficulty communicating due to cognitive changes or physical health issues such as hearing loss. If you're having trouble speaking with a loved one, contact their doctor for services that can assist. For example, if they have trouble hearing you, consult their doctor about whether hearing aids could be beneficial. If your loved one has serious hearing loss, you might also check into sign language training programs for you and them.

In addition, doctors and other healthcare professionals working with older people may have received training in coping with communication challenges.

Seek the help of family and friends. Caring for an older relative on your own may be exhausting. If you require assistance, do not hesitate to contact your support network. Discuss with relatives and friends how they may assist. For example, you may ask one of your siblings whether they would mind taking turns doing grocery shopping or domestic tasks. It might also be beneficial to have someone to vent to. Even if a friend or relative cannot provide physical assistance, they may be able to provide a sympathetic ear when needed. Consider the person's talents and resources while asking for assistance. For example, if your aunt enjoys cooking, you may invite her to assist you in preparing meals for your grandma on occasion.

Self-care is essential for preventing caregiver burnout. You won't be able to care for a loved one if you don't take care of yourself first. Make time to consume healthy foods, take care of your health, and do activities you love, such as working on hobbies or spending time with friends. If you're having difficulty finding time to care for yourself, ask a family or friend to fill in for you for a bit so you can take a break. For example, you may request that your brother stays with your mother for the evening so you can go out with friends. If you require a longer break, you might be able to find respite care in your region. If you can't afford respite care, look for community-based volunteer groups in your area.[43]

---

[43] "Generosity - Definition, Meaning & Synonyms | Vocabulary.com." https://www.vocabulary.com/dictionary/generosity.

Many people must begin caring for elderly loved ones at some point. When that time comes for your family, you want to ensure that the older person is treated with dignity, compassion, and patience. While the transition may be difficult for you, keep in mind that it is not simple for your loved one to become dependent on you or others for their care. Becoming acquainted with several methods of providing the finest treatment possible may be beneficial. Several methods assist the older person in your life feel secure and cared for. While it may appear daunting at first, providing care can make you feel more connected during this latter period of life.

Your loved one requires social contact with you. And by paying a visit, you may be certain they are safe, healthy, and doing well. It's usually a good idea to look about their house for any faults that need to be repaired during your visit. For example, you may want to inspect the overall cleanliness of the house or whether anything is broken and needs to be repaired. Check their food supplies, laundry, mail, and plants regularly. Finally, ascertain that your loved one has an appropriate prescription supply. All of their medicines must be filled and replenished as needed. With medicine, acquiring a pill box organizer with divisions labeled by day and AM and PM dosage is a good idea. This can assist in making their medication-taking procedure easier.

Engaging a helper, assistant, or another older adult caregiver may be necessary. This might be someone who assists your loved one with everyday tasks like showering, errands, or housework. You should always verify references or go via a registered agent if you don't know the person. This might be a charge included in your family budget or a service provided for free or at a minimal fee (depending on available resources).

When caring for older folks, it is essential to look around the house carefully and analyze what may be a safety threat. Some improvements may be easy, while others may be more complicated. These might include:

- Checking the general lighting in the house to ensure it is enough.

- Putting up an elevated toilet.

- Putting in a wheelchair or walker ramp.

- Handrails and grab bars for the toilet and shower.

- Ensure that any cables, cords, and wires are properly stowed away to avoid potential falls.

- Including non-slip mats or strips in the shower, bathtub, and any other potentially slippery parts of the house.

- They installed a few auto-sensor nightlights throughout the house to see if they woke up in the middle of the night.

- We are getting rid of any excess junk or furniture that is in the way.

- It was removing tiny carpets or those with high edges that might cause stumbling or catch on walkers/canes.

An older adult loved one may be uncomfortable or unwilling to discuss their money. However, you should strive to have open talks about their financial requirements and costs, especially if they are on a limited salary or have a budget to follow. While attending to the particular requirements of an aging loved one in the present, you may want to ensure that you are also prepared for the future. Regarding their vital documentation, ensure everything is up to date and finished. This might involve talking about their will or agreeing on power of attorney. These discussions might be difficult, but they are necessary to ensure that your loved one is prepared. Then, when the work is over, you will both have peace of mind.

Your loved one may eventually be unable to drive owing to deterioration in their eyesight or reaction times. It is critical to analyze their driving ability and, if necessary, suggest other solutions that may be beneficial. Consider hiring a driver or employing a grocery delivery service, for example. It is critical to keep older people active, and participating in Exercise is essential while caring for older loved ones since it keeps them healthy and reduces their risk of falling. Unfortunately, it is common for older people to become isolated, lonely, or even depressed, particularly if they have lost their spouses. People must maintain contact with their family and friends and adventure out to develop new relationships. You may be able to find resources in your area that might help keep your loved one social and active.

It is critical for their health that they are adequately nourished. Even if your schedule does not allow you to make meals daily, you may plan a few meals ahead of time. Furthermore, depending on their condition, your loved one may be eligible for assisted meal programs such as Meals on Wheels, or they may opt to sign up for a different meal plan. Some meal plans may even meet particular demands, such as diabetic meals. When caring for aging loved ones, there are several ways to use technology to your benefit. You may, for example, install a camera or a motion sensor to keep an eye on them while you are gone. A camera system can help you keep track of falls, how much they move, and other crucial information. Other technologies that your elderly loved one might utilize to notify you if something is wrong. One alternative is a Life Alert system, which includes a button your loved one may push to summon quick assistance. Using this method will necessitate convincing your loved one to wear it at all times in case of an accident.[44][45]

Working up a plan with other family members is important to assist your senior loved one with bathing, doctor appointments, errands, shopping, cooking, cleaning, and so on. If required, you may need to employ someone to assist with some of those duties to provide you and other family members with a respite from the continual demands of their schedule. A timetable helps you keep your life planned and organized and lets your loved ones know what's on their agenda. There are several resources for the elderly. These resources may be provided by the government or by the community and may include food stipends, exercise equipment, or transportation to doctor visits. Investigate what your loved one qualifies for and how it may assist them. What's accessible may surprise you.

To care for others, you must be physically and psychologically fit. Caregivers of elderly loved ones have been observed to have greater stress, anxiety, and depression rates. If feasible, distribute the responsibilities among yourself, your spouse, other family members, and anybody you trust who is willing to assist. Remember to take breaks, get away for a while, and enjoy your life. You may feel obligated to be there to care for the older adult in your life, but you must also be present for yourself and understand your own needs.

---

[44] "What Is Generosity? - The Spiritual Life." https://slife.org/generosity/.
[45] "Generosity Definition & Meaning | Dictionary.com." https://www.dictionary.com/browse/generosity.

How To Love Your Kids

Being a parent may be challenging. If you have children and want to learn how to better display and feel your love for them, you may change things up to make things simpler. Learn to love your children and be the best parent you can be by taking small actions. Everyone has characteristics that require extra effort to handle. However, it becomes simpler to understand human "weaknesses" as the inverse of our strengths. For example, a youngster may be extremely obstinate, battling with her parents until she simply wears them out. While the attribute is difficult to live with, the opposite side of the trait is tenacity. This perseverance will benefit this youngster if she grows up to be a scientist, author, or attorney; such perseverance would benefit practically any career. If this is our child, we can teach her that her perseverance is a strength, but it may also drive people insane and make them upset with her. She must learn to moderate and use it rather than allowing it to rule her. One of the most beneficial gifts any parent can offer a child is to assist them in getting to know themselves and contorting themselves to achieve their overall goals.

Maybe you wanted a male but ended up with a girl. Perhaps you expected a peaceful, compliant youngster but received an energetic live wire instead. Perhaps your child has particular needs that make parenting more difficult. Maybe you're disappointed she got your luxurious mane instead of that tangly curly mop. If there is something you wish was different about your child, they will most certainly notice. The knowledge may not be expressed in words but via a visceral sensation of not being good enough. The remedy is to allow oneself to feel those emotions and to grieve. Allow it to go. Grief burns, yet it purifies the soul and allows us to accept what is.

From there, we may accept our genuine children rather than an idealized version of who they should be.

Naturally, we assume we're correct...which means our child is incorrect. Alternatively, and in a sense that is far more grounded in reality: Your child's "misbehavior" is an SOS. There is always a cause, an unhappy emotion, or an unfulfilled need behind your child's misbehaving. Address the root problem, not the behavior, and you'll see a difference in your child – because you responded to her SOS. When youngsters act out, they are informing us — in the only way they know how at the time — that they need our assistance. Misbehavior becomes understandable and tolerable when we see it through the eyes of our children. The barriers to love dissolve, and our love becomes unconditional. Control your rage. Unconditional love says that the kid feels the parent's love without needing to do anything, even behave. Did he strike his younger sister? Did she slam the door and yell, "I hate you!"? Did he throw something at your head? Did she have a meltdown at the restaurant? It's difficult to love our children when they drive us insane. As a result, we fail. Of course, we know we adore them anyway. However, if you question the child, they do not feel loved.[46][47]

Will your fury, however, teach your child the lesson you intend? When our children misbehave, the most effective solution is to establish a clear, calm limit and then love our child through his distress. When we give in to our rage, we model bad conduct to our children. And children do misinterpret our rage. At best, they

---

[46] "What is Generosity? - Faith+Lead." 28 Jul. 2015, https://faithlead.luthersem.edu/what-is-generosity/.

[47] "Generosity – Concept, importance, examples and phrases." https://conceptdaily.com/generosity-concept-importance-examples-and-phrases/.

believe they are awful individuals who will never be good enough. What about heavy lifting? Yes. It takes continuous work to develop this type of cardiac muscle. But there is nothing more satisfying. These five behaviors will bring you and your kid closer together, her conduct will improve tremendously, and she will know for the rest of her life that she is more than enough just the way she is. That is being genuinely loved. Unconditionally.

Taking Little Steps

Simply be with your children; do not "parent" them. Many parents are scared by the role they must play. When you have a child, there is a lot of pressure to be a parent with a capital "P." Instead of thinking about what that entails, create your position. Being a parent does not imply that you must raise a flawless child or be a perfect person. Simply be yourself. Instead of focusing on the hardship of parenting, consider the opportunity. Every day, you get to hang around with bizarre little beings that you made. You get to converse with a youngster who sees the world for the first time. You're quite fortunate. Take a step back from your children and observe them. Enjoy the time they're experiencing for themselves.

Play with your children. Get down in the soil with your kids and talk to them about what they're doing, even if it appears like they're poking an acorn with a stick they've just drooled on. Learn how to use the Xbox. Keep track of all the strange TV shows they wish to watch. Discover what makes people tick. Simply ask them questions about what they're doing or remark, "What's that?" while playing or pretending. Get them to talk. If they have any queries, be available to answer them. Take your children seriously. Use your performance as a negotiating chip to get things done. Saying something like, "I'll play with you for the next 15 minutes, and then we can get your room cleaned up, okay?" works far better for everyone than shouting.

Every day, communicate with your children. According to studies, children who are spoken to more frequently while developing have a greater success rate and a track record of happiness than children who are spoken to less frequently. Pay attention to your children. Just chat, even if they aren't saying anything. You also don't have to talk to them about trivial matters. Tell them about your experience at work. Listen to what people say, even if it doesn't make much sense at the moment. Encourage your children to speak out when they have something to say. Inquire about your children's interests and attempt to comprehend or get interested in them. Find activities that you both like doing together.[48]

They should be worn out. A child who is calm and sleepy is an easy child to adore. Kids who have had a long day are much easier to manage. Everyone benefits. So, instead of plopping your kids in front of the TV, keep them occupied with hobbies and things to do. Take your children to the park regularly to let them play. It will be an experience for them, and you will let them exhaust their energies. The phrase "like a baby in the mall" has been used several times. When you can conduct a fast sensory-overload event, your kids will be exhausted. So go shopping with them. Bring them to the shop. It may be a difficult hour for you, but you can take a thirty-minute nap later.

Alter their diet. Some people feel that diets high in processed foods and artificial colors might cause behavioral and attention problems.

---

[48] "Generosity - Wikipedia." https://en.wikipedia.org/wiki/Generosity.

While there is no definitive evidence that food causes illnesses such as ADHD, there are several reasons why eliminating processed and refined sugars from your children's diet and increasing their intake of fresh fruits and vegetables may be beneficial. When children behave out, it is sometimes because their blood sugar is low. Give your children nutritious food if they are misbehaving. Snack time is a simple method to provide nutritious meals to your children. Feed your children some apple slices or a handful of almonds. Make ants-on-a-stick. Something healthy. Take family dinners together. Make it a habit to sit at the table together every night.[49]

Put down your phone. If you want your children to be quieter, speak to them quietly and make your house peaceful. Being louder will not benefit anyone but will only make children louder. Have someone you can contact if you are stressed. Things can get difficult at times. You're trying to cook supper or do something essential, but your kids won't stop shouting or fighting. Yikes. When you've reached your breaking point, it's a good idea to call someone and speak it out. This can be a lifesaver. Discuss it with a family member or close friend who has children. There may be no answer, but simply talking to someone else might be a relief. Tell them what your children are doing that irritates you. Let it all out. Keep the number of a babysitter handy in case you need a break. The ultimate irony? Parenting is a never-ending process. If you're experiencing problems with your children, call your parent and speak out. Allow them to lend a sympathetic ear.

---

[49] "Generosity - definition of generosity by The Free Dictionary."
https://www.thefreedictionary.com/generosity.

Being A Good Parent

Stop correcting your children until it is really necessary. Your role as a parent is not to be a never-ending supply of wisdom. Allow them to sort things out for themselves and make their errors. Allow your children to scratch their knees. Please don't give your youngsters advice on making their construction stronger. Don't teach them how to make a better tower. Instead, show your support and interest in what they're doing. If you want to do it correctly, make your statue. When it comes to counsel, try to give your children the benefit of the doubt. Their songs will most likely sound awful to you. Their favorite movies will almost certainly be unbearably horrible as yours were most likely to your parents. If your child is doing anything risky, respond gently but forcefully. Be open and honest with them about the repercussions of risky behavior. Be kind to your children. Let's face it: kids can be a pain. You may still love and parent your children properly and express it. However, learning to be patient with your children and allowing them to act like children can help you love them more. Expect them to grate on your nerves. Expect them to behave like children. Things will go much more smoothly. Choose your battles wisely and be the greater person. Don't allow your children to manipulate you into being annoyed. If they're getting on your nerves, talk to them or offer them something else to do.

Discipline your children with love. Discipline must be implemented quickly, calmly, firmly, and consistently. Discipline your children only when required, and do so consistently. Take a step back whenever you feel yourself becoming enraged. If you suspect you're punishing your child because you're upset or frustrated with anything else, sit quietly for five or ten minutes. If necessary, speak with someone. When your children discover something they enjoy, coach them. Please encourage your children to pursue their interests: painting, basketball, football, soccer, or anything else they enjoy. Encourage them, learn everything you can about their interest and assist them along the way. Coach them in something they enjoy rather than something you enjoy. Have you always desired to be a world-class soccer player but lacked the necessary skills? If your child is interested, that's fantastic. If your child wants to play the guitar, don't make them do anything else.

Respect your children's personal space. Each of your children must have something they are accountable for and can call their own. Allow them to make decorating selections and care for their place. Even if you don't have enough space for your children to have their bedroom, it's still crucial for them to have their area. Assign tasks to your children. Respect your child's privacy and their decisions. Believe in your parenting abilities and believe you raised them to make good decisions.[50][51]

Taking Time For Yourself

Create a schedule to give yourself a break from parenting. Every parent requires a break from the action. It's beneficial to incorporate some break into your daily schedule to allow yourself to unwind and relax from your parenting responsibilities. Make it a rule that if your children see you reading a favorite magazine or taking up a book, they will not bother you for fifteen minutes. Tell them that if they are, they may have a snack afterward—baths, in a nutshell. If you've

---

[50] "How to Love Your Kids (with Pictures) - wikiHow." 06 May. 2021, https://www.wikihow.com/Love-Your-Kids.

[51] "35 Simple Ways To Love Your Child In Everyday Life." https://amotherfarfromhome.com/love-your-child/.

been caring for children all day, treat yourself to a 15-minute bath at the end. Well-deserved. Make play dates. Make an arrangement with other parents to take your kids for a couple of hours in the afternoon, and then volunteer to do the same at regular intervals. If you want to love your children and spend time with them after being refreshed and relaxed, you need to take a break from parenting. Allow your children some alone time if they are older or too old for playdates. Allow them to roam the neighborhood. Allow them some leeway.

Regularly hire a sitter. A few hours away at night may be quite beneficial. Make it a habit to hire a babysitter regularly so you can go out and have fun with your partner or yourself. Experiencing life without children may be an eye-opening experience. When you go out, enlist the assistance of others. Bring someone with you if taking your children out in public is tough. With the knowledge that you'll have the company of an important person in your life when you go out, you'll be more likely to enjoy yourself. If you dread a large shopping excursion with your kids, carry some backup.

Stop circling. Being a parent might be more stressful than enjoyable at times. If you're continuously anxious about your children and working hard to ensure their success, it might be time to let go. Stop lingering and take a step back. Allow them to live their own lives and make their errors. They'll be OK. In certain locations, a new parenting philosophy known as "free-range kids" is gaining popularity. It entails providing children greater independence than we generally consider proper. Would you let a youngster under 10 take the metro alone? Or skateboard alone in another section of town? Some individuals do. Teach your children the basic safety guidelines and trust them to behave responsibly.[52][53][54][55]

[52] "12 Ways to Love Your Wayward Child | Desiring God." 09 May. 2007, https://www.desiringgod.org/articles/12-ways-to-love-your-wayward-child.

[53] "5 Secrets to Love Your Child Unconditionally | Psychology Today." 02 Mar. 2014, https://www.psychologytoday.com/us/blog/peaceful-parents-happy-kids/201403/5-secrets-love-your-child-unconditionally.

[54] "How to Love Your Kids Unconditionally - Crosswalk.com." 02 Apr. 2013, https://www.crosswalk.com/family/parenting/teens/how-to-love-your-kids-unconditionally.html.

[55] "Teaching Children How To Love - freemansperspective.com." 31 Jan. 2022, https://freemansperspective.com/teaching-children-how-to-love/.

CHAPTER-4

How To Cultivate Self-Sacrifice Habits

Every sacrifice made for the sake of others brings divine delight. People who do not make sacrifices for other people will be forgotten as soon as they die. Some individuals live eternally even after death because "we live in actions, not years"; duration of life is evaluated not by the number of years one lives but by the good deeds done during one's life. Human life is a gift from the Almighty (SWT) and has a temporal limit. The ultimate eternal truth is death. If we are unable to help others, our lives are meaningless. If anyone remembers him, it will be for his selfish attitudes and vices. Our life should be built on good actions and qualities.

The word "sacrifice" is frequently connected with the apparent loss of something worthwhile. Sacrifice may take various forms, including sacrificing time, labor, riches, desires, pleasure, and even life for the happiness and safety of others. The actual worth of sacrifice may not be felt as deeply by the one doing it until the rewards of their sacrifice are visible or expressed. We must make compromises to accomplish what we truly desire in life. Small actions such as being nice and courteous to others, assisting the needy, and spending money on the education of poor children, among others, are examples of noble deeds that may be done daily. Selfless behaviors, gestures, and deeds abound throughout human existence. We must all endeavor to make the best of the great gift of life. We should remember that one packed hour of a magnificent life is worth more than a year of doing good.[56]

When we surrender something valuable, we do not always truly lose it. We're simply passing it off to someone else. Without suffering and sacrifice, we would have nothing. However, holiness and pain are not incompatible. In other words, holiness does not imply that you will be devoid of pain in your life. However, it does imply that your pain will be altered. Consider the life of Jesus Himself. He was flawless. He, on the other hand, suffered the most. The greatest of all human beings, Prophet Muhammad (SM), suffered unimaginable agony. Instead of suffering as an indication of disapproval from God, it is a normal part of a life of radical discipleship in an imperfect world.

Our lives are all about choices; we get to choose what we're prepared to give up to obtain the things we value the most. We will not obtain what we deserve if we are unwilling to make sacrifices. Many believe that the world revolves around their comfort, preferences, and pleasure. Sacrifice improves self-control. It is also a form of

---

[56] "6 Practical Ways to Show Unconditional Love to Kids." 12 Feb. 2020, https://www.thearkgroup.org/blog/unconditional-love.

penance. It can also be used to express regret. Many individuals seek enjoyment in it and have to push themselves to do so. Sacrifice has diverse meanings for different individuals. Contributors and recipients may be unaware of the outcome of their combined or individual actions. Survivors of wars know how hard warriors fight to win and go above and beyond the odds to save their fellow soldiers' lives. There is no appropriate benefit without sacrifice.

A conscientious learner free of materialistic hunger is also a form of sacrifice. Comfort, delight, and enjoyment are all sacrificed. He will be richly compensated sooner or later. Many individuals nowadays have illusions about sacrifice; they believe it would reduce their money and disrupt their enjoyment. On the contrary, it aids in the removal of all obstructions to living a calm existence. It may hurt us at first, but we eventually appreciate it. It can only be comprehended if someone makes a sacrifice. The world's most successful people have made the greatest sacrifices. Prayer is the fruit of quiet, faith is the fruit of prayer, love is the fruit of love, service is the fruit of service, and peace is the fruit of service.

We must sometimes make sacrifices to advance. The incapacity to make sacrifices for others is one of the leading reasons for failure in our lives. On the other hand, the power of sacrifice may transform lives and has enormous global significance. As a result, we must learn to sacrifice and pursue deeper truths in life. Every connection in our lives, whether romantic, marital or otherwise, necessitates some sacrifice to attain success and happiness. Still, partnerships thrive when we develop mutual dependency and construct something greater together than we would have separately. Every man dies for what he believes, and every woman dies for what she believes. Unfortunately, people sometimes believe in little or nothing, so they devote their life little or nothing.[57][58]

If we wish to win the trust and respect of people, we must first earn it by our actions. It has been proved that no one wants to befriend or work with someone whose self-centered and selfish. Good individuals make sacrifices for the happiness of others. We see something wonderful happen when we are prepared to give anything to others. People with strong moral integrity make sacrifices for the greater good, whether for their neighbors or family. They give freely of themselves without regard for personal benefit because they are as invested in the success of others as they are in their own. Parents labor and forgo rest to guarantee that the family may continue to thrive. A parent suffers from burnout and exhaustion to secure their child's well-being. A teacher devotes time away from their children to the growth of others. An entrepreneur donates revenues to a local charity so the community can finally thrive. In our lives, there is no rewind button. We should see life as one large adventure with many excursions at various periods. The quest for knowledge will likely last a lifetime, running concurrently to other journeys such as maturity, work, family rearing, etc. There is a perfect reward for every journey we take, even if it is fraught with the stress of daily life.

---

[57] "How to Explain Love to Little Kids - Fatherly." 13 Feb. 2018, https://www.fatherly.com/love-money/how-to-explain-love-to-little-kids.
[58] "3 Ways to Be Loved by Little Kids - wikiHow." 05 Aug. 2020, https://www.wikihow.com/Be-Loved-by-Little-Kids.

The Path To Altruism

It's more than simply a nice idea to serve others without concern for ourselves. Selflessness improves the quality and purpose of our lives and the lives of our offspring; in fact, our very existence may rely on it. Serving others without concern for one's well-being is more than an admirable ideal. Selflessness improves the quality and purpose of our lives and the lives of our offspring; in fact, our very existence may rely on it. We must have the clarity to see this and the courage to say so.

Humanity has three major challenges: providing adequate living circumstances for everybody, increasing life enjoyment, and conserving our planet. Because these needs cover multiple time horizons, traditional cost-benefit analysis struggles to reconcile them. We are concerned about the status of the economy from year to year, but we think about our pleasure throughout a lifetime. Still, our concern for the environment will mostly help future generations. However, a charitable method necessitates minimal trade-offs. Regardless of the possible reward for himself, a prudent investor will never gamble with his client's life savings. A concerned citizen will consider how his activities will affect his community first. A selfless generation will take care of the globe to leave a sustainable world for its descendants. Altruism benefits everyone.

This worldview may appear utopian. After all, psychology, economics, and evolutionary biology have all asserted that humans are fundamentally selfish. However, research over the last 30 years shows that real altruism may extend beyond kin and community to include the well-being of humans and other animals. Furthermore, the altruist does not have to suffer due to his good activities; on the contrary, he gains indirectly from them, whereas the selfish actor frequently causes sorrow for himself and others. Individuals can also learn to be altruistic, according to research. Neuroscientists have discovered three components of altruism that everyone can learn: empathy (understanding and sharing another's feelings), loving-kindness (the desire to share happiness), and compassion (a desire to relieve the suffering of another).

Societies can also grow more altruistic (and may even enjoy an evolutionary advantage over their more selfish counterparts). According to cultural evolution research, our values can change faster than our DNA. Therefore, we must recognize the value of altruism, cultivate it in ourselves, and create a cultural transformation to make the world a better place.

The necessity for cultivating this recognition is now more apparent than in our economic system. The ideological goal of infinite quantitative expansion puts unsustainable stresses on our world and exacerbates inequality. However, reversing that expansion would cause other issues; forcing people to fight for shrinking goods and resources would increase unemployment, poverty, and possibly violence.

So a compromise must be struck: the global community must pull 1.5 billion people out of poverty while limiting the excesses of the world's richest consumers. They are responsible for the great bulk of environmental destruction. Raising taxes isn't necessary; instead, we may persuade the wealthy that their standard of living isn't improved by chasing after more money. This notion of "sustainable harmony" may be promoted by releasing, alongside regular GDP statistics, measures of human well-being and environmental preservation. Bhutan's government, for example, already accounts for its people's "social wealth" and "natural wealth" in addition to GDP data.

Along with standard securities markets, we may create a stock exchange comprised of so-called ethical organizations such as social companies, cooperative banks, microcredit agencies, and fair-trade groups. Several efforts have made tiny steps in this direction, including those in Brazil, South Africa, and the United Kingdom. Small steps result in enormous improvements. As the benefits of altruism become more apparent, the new strategy will expand across the economy, benefiting everyone, future generations, and the planet.

How To Become A Effective Altruist

Effective altruism is a social movement and a philosophy that seeks to increase charitable donations of time and money and to encourage the most effective use of these resources, typically by focusing on measurable impacts such as lives saved per dollar. The essential question for a successful altruist is, "Of all the conceivable ways to make a difference, how can I make the largest impact?" For example, it may be claimed that charity work isn't the greatest use of time; a smart financier could be better suited to working for a bank and using their profits to pay others to work for charities instead. To that purpose, members of the movement typically do sophisticated calculations to determine which charities and vocations do the most good, which is usually criticized. Charities such as the ALS Association, which profited from the viral ice bucket challenge, and the arts are examples of charitable organizations that effective altruists think should be prioritized lower on our list of priorities.[59][60]

These comparisons are based on the cost-to-benefit ratio, not the merit of the cause, the good it causes, or even the amount of suffering it alleviates. For example, Peter Singer, a moral philosopher and hero of the effective altruism movement, has suggested that in the rich world, homelessness and infant mortality should be prioritized lower than analogous problems in the poor world. It's not because these issues are insignificant or unnecessary, but because they have a higher impact per dollar. In many respects, Effective Altruism is exciting and useful. It starts individuals thinking about how they can help others and inspires them to act in ways that help others. Unfortunately, many people do not contribute as much as they should, sometimes because they are unsure whether their efforts will make a difference or where to focus them. While we support the movement, determining certain reasons are superior to others risks oversimplification. Instead, here are five practical strategies to become a truly effective altruist.

This is unarguable and is already a core premise of effective altruism. We can all agree that waste and harm are terrible, and many philanthropic activities create more harm than benefit. Therefore, let's avoid them. However, many selfless actions accomplish some good — frequently a lot of good — even if they are not the greatest. Different people may contribute in various ways and support many important initiatives. Choosing merely the best

---

[59] "15 Ways You Can Show Your Kids You Love Them — Every Day." 25 Jun. 2018, https://www.huffpost.com/entry/15-ways-you-can-show-your-kids-you-love-themevery_b_5b1ac57be4b0253c28270715.
[60] "5 Ways to Show Love to Your Children - for the family." https://forthefamily.org/5-ways-show-love-children/.

gives little room for originality and exploration and might turn off many individuals. Volunteers for Habitat for Humanity should not be unable to construct strong dwellings. And they do not volunteer at the RSPCA if they do not love dealing with animals. The same is true for monetary gifts. If the greatest good my money can do is to help free animals on factory farms, but I don't care about these creatures, I'm unlikely to contribute as much, as frequently, or for as long as I would for a cause that I feel profound about. The notion that we should labor for or donate to the most effective charity, regardless of our interests, is self-defeating. Most people's passions aren't so adaptable; they can't or won't start caring about a cause just because a formula says they should. It is preferable to pursue a passion than to get demotivated.[61]

Encourage people if you are truly committed to a cause. If they aren't enthusiastic about your cause, urge them to help others in other ways. We can do more to better the world if we enlist the aid of others. We'd get different responses if we tried to figure out who did the most good in history. Effective altruism can come through motivating others, such as being a good teacher or parent. Take, for example, Singer. He hasn't avoided nuclear war or cured smallpox but has inspired many people to assist others. In turn, these followers have followers who aid others more than they would have otherwise. A teacher should be credited for the good that his students perform that they would not have done otherwise. We may help others both directly and indirectly by motivating them.

If someone is doing more good than others but could yet do more, they deserve to be praised and encouraged. To inspire individuals

---

[61] "Four Parenting Tips on How to Love Your Children Equally." 26 May. 2020, https://goodlifedetroit.com/parenting-tips-love-your-children-equally/.

to improve, we should praise those who go above and beyond and heap even more praise on those near the top. Criticizing individuals who fall short of the standard simply serves to discourage others. If we are correct, condemnation should be saved for those who go much below what most people do to aid the poor. True altruism seeks to accomplish the most benefit over the long term. The world, both current and future, is a dangerous place. It is impossible to forecast what will be most beneficial today or in the future. In the face of such uncertainty, humility is required. Who could have predicted that the development of the cell phone would be so beneficial, or who knows what the long-term impact of the communications revolution will be? As philosopher John Stuart Mill recognized, creativity, diversity, and live experiments are required to find what is the ideal existence. The same is true for other people's well-being. Be open to revising your objectives in light of fresh facts and thinking.[62][63]

---

[62] "13 Ways To Raise Kids Who Love And Care For Each Other." https://www.lifehack.org/articles/lifestyle/13-ways-raise-kids-who-love-and-care-for-each-other.html.
[63] "16 Parenting Rules That Teach Us How to Really Love a Child." 11 Mar. 2022, https://www.creativehealthyfamily.com/how-to-really-love-a-child-parenting/.

CHAPTER-5

Analysis Of Your Attitude

How To Build A Positive Attitude

A good mindset is essential for living a full and joyful life. Developing a good attitude can help you identify and reflect on happy feelings when they arise. You will also begin reframing unpleasant feelings as soon as they arise. Taking care of oneself and nurturing relationships are critical components of a healthy mindset. Having a positive attitude is difficult, but keeping it can sometimes be difficult. Once you've discovered a positive attitude, the stresses of daily life, sad occurrences in the news, and all the incoming negativity might feel like the world is attempting to pull you down. Maintain your optimism by thinking positively, feeling positive, and doing positively. You will gain stronger interpersonal interactions, more creativity, simpler decision-making, and higher enjoyment if you can tap into and sustain positive thinking.

Understanding The Importance Of A Positive Attitude

Recognize that a happy attitude reduces bad feelings. An optimistic mindset will allow you to experience many happy feelings. These are the times when bad feelings don't weigh you down. It can properly speed up the healing process after a traumatic experience. Recognize the connection between pleasant emotions and physical well-being. According to research, stress and other unpleasant emotions might lead to health problems such as coronary heart disease. It can increase your general well-being by replacing negative emotions with good ones. Positive emotions can help decrease illness development. This is since good emotions reduce the duration of negative emotional arousal. Connect happiness, creativity, and focus. A happy attitude generates a "broad, flexible cognitive structure and capacity to assimilate varied material" and physical benefits. These effects are connected to higher amounts of dopamine in the brain, improving your attention, creativity, and learning capacity. Positive emotions also boost a person's capacity to deal with adversity. Recover more rapidly from bad life situations. Developing and maintaining a good attitude might help you be more resilient in the face of adversity, such as trauma or grief. People who experience pleasant feelings throughout grieving are more likely to make sound long-term goals. A year following a loss, having objectives and ambitions may result in a higher sense of well-being. Participants in an experiment on emotional resilience and stress reactions were given a demanding assignment to complete. The findings revealed that all individuals felt apprehensive about the job regardless of their resilience. However, the more robust individuals recovered to a calmer state faster than the less resilient people.[64]

Taking Time For Self-Reflection

Accept that change takes time. Consider establishing a good attitude like you would consider improving strength or athleticism. It is a long-term project that needs regular work. Identify and cultivate your best qualities. To assist more good emotional experiences, focus on your talents. As a result, dealing with hardship will be easier. Make a list of activities you like to do or are skilled at. Try to accomplish some of these things regularly. This will increase your stock of happy experiences. Create a diary. According to research, self-reflection may be an effective learning and teaching technique at school and work. Self-reflection can also aid in the development of a happy mindset. Writing down your feelings and ideas might assist you in recognizing your actions and reactions. Writing self-reflections may appear unusual or awkward at first. However, with time and experience, you will begin to see behavioral and emotional patterns in your writing. This can help you discover areas that may obstruct your progress toward your goals. Write down the good things that happened to you today. Examine the day and look for good aspects. Things that make you joyful, proud, awed, appreciative, serene, satisfied, delighted, or any other pleasant emotion can be included.

Consider your morning routine, and pay attention when you feel quiet or cheerful. This may be a lovely view on your daily drive, enjoying your first cup of coffee, or a pleasant discussion. Spend

---

[64] "How to Love Your Child When You Can't Even Love Yourself - Purpose Fairy." https://www.purposefairy.com/97372/love-your-child-love-yourself/.

time reflecting on when you were proud of yourself or thankful to someone else. These might be little gestures, such as thanking your partner for making the bed. You may also be proud of how you finished a chore or a challenge you set for yourself. You might find it useful to begin your thoughts with the highlights of your day. Reliving happy feelings might help you modify your perspective on unfavorable experiences. Write about times when you had bad feelings. Identify times during your day when you had unpleasant feelings. Examples are guilt, humiliation, embarrassment, frustration, disappointment, fear, or contempt. Do any of these ideas strike you as outlandish? Maybe you're embarrassed about spilling coffee on your boss. Do you believe you'll be fired as a result of the event and will never be able to find work again? Extreme reactions to regular events might stifle more constructive, useful thought.

Reframe bad experiences as beneficial. Examine your list of unpleasant experiences. Spend time reframing these events so that you may get good (or at least neutral) feelings from them. For example, if you had road rage on your way home, reframe the other driver's intentions as a genuine error. If you were humiliated by something that happened during the day, consider how stupid or humorous the event was. Even though your boss was unhappy because coffee was spilled on him, errors happen. Hopefully, your manager will find the fun in it as well. You can manage problems better if you do not perceive little blunders as life-changing events. One method to address the coffee scenario is to exhibit genuine worry for your boss's safety and that you did not burn him. You can then offer to purchase him another shirt during your lunch break or dry-clean the soiled one. Use your "happy reserves." Over time, improved coping abilities lead to an increase in pleasant feelings. The advantages of experiencing positive emotions are long-lasting.

They persist significantly longer than the duration of your delight. You may access your "happy reserves" anytime and in any emotional condition.[65][66]

Don't be concerned if you're having difficulty creating pleasant emotional experiences. You may also use your memories to replenish your "happy reserves." Remember that everyone has problems in life. It's vital to realize that everyone has little major life challenges, so you're not alone. It takes skill to reframe your excessive responses and time to modify and accept. However, with experience, you may be able to let go of little details. You'll be able to look at larger difficulties objectively and perceive them as learning opportunities. Control your inner critic. Your "inner critic" might hamper your efforts to cultivate a good mindset. For example, suppose your inner critic labeled you stupid for spilling coffee on your boss. Your inner critic constantly criticizes you and is mean to you. Consider how often your inner critic says stuff like these. When your inner critic comes out, you will acquire better insight into the problems. You might also fight your inner critic and other negative thinking habits. This is an essential component in developing a good attitude.

Taking Time For Yourself

Do things you like. Spend time doing activities that provide you joy or pleasure. It might be difficult to make time for oneself, especially if you are someone who prioritizes others. It may also be difficult if

---

[65] "72 Incredibly Simple Ways to Show Love for Children." 10 Feb. 2021, https://parentswithconfidence.com/72-incredibly-simple-ways-to-show-love-for-children/.

[66] "HOW TO LOVE A CHILD - Janusz Korczak." http://www.januszkorczak.ca/legacy/3_How%20to%20Love%20a%20Child.pdf.

you have a living situation such as small children at home or are caring for someone unwell. However, "secure your oxygen mask before aiding others." When you are your best self, you are the best caregiver. Listen to music if it makes you joyful. If reading books makes you joyful, set aside some time to read in a peaceful setting. Gaze at gorgeous scenery, visit a museum, or watch a movie you like. Continue to engage in activities that offer you joy. This is an excellent method for concentrating on the good. No one else observes or criticizes your assessment of your day and yourself, so there is no need to be concerned about appearing arrogant. It is unnecessary to be good at something or to please others to enjoy it. If you enjoy cooking, tell yourself that you are a talented cook. Similarly, you don't have to be able to lure forest creatures to enjoy singing. Observing moments of pleasure, pride, happiness, or delight in your life, as well as the actions that bring them about, is an excellent method to ensure that you can repeat them in the future.[67][68][69]

Be less concerned about others. Because you are not like other people, there is no reason to judge yourself by their standards. You may appreciate activities that others do not. You are undoubtedly "allowed" to construct your definition of success in your life. Try not to compare yourself to others. Your perception of yourself differs greatly from that of others, just as watching a Monet painting from one foot away differs greatly from viewing it from twenty feet away.

---

[67] "11 Simple Ways to Show Your Child Your Love - Parents." 02 Mar. 2022, https://www.parents.com/parenting/better-parenting/simple-ways-to-show-your-child-your-love/.

[68] "100 Ways to Show Your Children You Love Them Deeply." 26 Aug. 2021, https://joannabel.com/100-ways-to-show-your-children-you-love-them/.

[69] "How to Love like a Child | HuffPost Communities." 30 Jan. 2013, https://www.huffpost.com/entry/how-to-love_b_2537774.

Please recognize that the picture you perceive of someone else may be a fabricated image they are attempting to convey. This picture may only be a partial representation of reality. Let go of comparing yourself to others and basing your self-worth on their opinions. This will allow you to draw fewer subjective conclusions about other people's actions. For example, if you have unpleasant contact with a casual acquaintance, don't assume they don't like you. Instead, presume that there was a misunderstanding between the two of you or that something else is bothering your acquaintance.

Cultivating Relationships

Maintain positive relationships. There is no doubt that relationships are a vital part of the human experience, even if you consider yourself an "introvert," someone who recharges by spending time alone and does not necessitate having many close friends. Friendships and partnerships provide support, affirmation, and strength to people of all genders and types. Maintain good relationships with family and friends throughout your life. According to research, chatting with someone you care about and receiving a supportive reaction from them may immediately enhance your attitude. Create new relationships. Identify the folks that make you feel wonderful to be around when you meet new people. Develop relationships with them. These folks will strengthen your support network and assist you in maintaining a happy mindset. Talk about your emotions with a buddy. If you're having trouble producing pleasant emotional experiences on your own, get help from a buddy. You should not feel obligated to bury your bad feelings. Instead, discussing them with a buddy might help you resolve them and make place for other positive feelings.

Handling Stressful Situations

Put a good spin on a negative situation. Positively reappraising a difficult situation is taking that scenario and giving it a fresh spin. For example, instead of looking at your to-do list and saying, "There's no way I can get all of this done," try stating, "I can get most of this done." Try problem-solving coping. Problem-focused coping involves concentrating on the source of your stress and devising a solution. Break the problem down into steps that will help you to complete it. Determine probable stumbling barriers and how you will deal with them when they occur. For example, if you have difficulty getting a group of coworkers to work effectively, sit down and examine the scenario. [70][71]

Determine the sorts of scenarios that are occurring. Then, think and write down potential solutions to these issues. For example, Jeff dislikes Sally, and your employer discourages collaboration and instead encourages individual achievements. Using problem-focused coping, you should declare that, while Jeff and Sally are permitted to dislike each other, a professional standard of behavior is required, and you should reinforce those norms. Then do a group activity in which everyone speaks three kind things about each other. Your team may act as an example to help transform the culture in your organization by connecting team members and executing tasks with resounding success. Finally, find positive significance in everyday occurrences. Finding positive significance in commonplace happenings and inside the hardship itself is

---

[70] "How to achieve a positive attitude - Harvard Health." 12 Apr. 2017, https://www.health.harvard.edu/mind-and-mood/how-to-achieve-a-positive-attitude.

[71] "What Is the Meaning of Positive Attitude – Definitions." https://www.successconsciousness.com/blog/positive-attitude/what-is-the-meaning-of-positive-attitude/.

another way people feel pleasant emotions in the face of adversity. Remember that the more you practice putting a positive spin on a difficult circumstance, the easier and more natural it will become. As a result of this technique, your outlook on even the most challenging situations will be improved, and you'll have more fun.

Thinking Positive

Feed your brain with optimism. A lot of negativity seems to be around us these days, which has a detrimental effect on our mental state. Stop viewing or listening to TV, social media, or the news if it makes you feel like "the world is dreadful" or "there is so much evil out there." It will be simpler to keep a happy mindset if you change or counterbalance what you are allowing from negative to positive. Play music with upbeat lyrics and rhythms. Read novels and look for uplifting material. Follow organizations and websites encouraging optimism, such as Upworthy or Little Things. It is possible to attain your goals if you focus on the positive aspects of your situation. A positive mindset can alter how you process new thoughts, feelings, and events. Because your brain is like a muscle, you must train it even when you don't feel like it. Positive thinking may help you retain a positive mindset while providing other significant benefits.

- Lower levels of anxiety and depression rates
- increased longevity
- Improve your coping abilities during times of adversity.
- Immune system boost

Use the practice of positive reframing. It may be tough to maintain a cheerful attitude under stressful conditions. To aid you, a cognitive approach can help you change how you react to such circumstances. Positive reframing requests that you recognize bad occurrences or damaging beliefs and make a deliberate choice to modify them or change how you view them. This strategy does not alter what is occurring but can alter how you feel, resulting in a more constant capacity to remain happy. In addition, any assumptions you have about yourself or your situation should be challenged.

When speaking, change your terminology. For example, change "He hates me and is only trying to drive me insane" to "Yes, he was not kind, but perhaps he is having a very rough day today."[72][73]

Exercise thankfulness. Being able to perceive the positive daily is the first step toward remaining positive. Think on and concentrate on the things you are thankful for by jotting down three new things you are grateful for that day. According to life coach Leah Morris, you may find optimism and thankfulness in the most difficult and stressful times of your life. Positive thinking and focusing on what you have rather than your lack can be aided by practicing gratitude. Make sure you enjoy both tiny and large joys. If you're still having trouble, you may buy gratitude notebooks online or use gratitude diary apps on your smartphone with suggestions to help you. Work on your thankfulness notebook at night so you may conclude each day with a pleasant mindset.

Redirect or minimize your negative ideas. You'll be powerless against your bad thoughts. Although you may train yourself to think

---

[72] "Positive Attitude: Definition, Examples, & Strategies."
https://www.berkeleywellbeing.com/develop-positive-attitude.html.
[73] "10 Creative Ways to Keep a Positive Attitude No Matter What." 29 Apr. 2021,
https://blog.hubspot.com/service/positive-attitude.

more positively, unpleasant thoughts will still come. When they do, you have the option of redirecting or limiting them. Set a time restriction of 5 minutes for engaging in negative thinking. Recognize it, give it time and space, then say enough and move on to positive thinking and reframing. Engage in a pleasant activity, such as assisting someone, phoning a friend, or exercising, until the negative thoughts pass. Sing your favorite songs, so the lyrics become your attention rather than negative thoughts.

Feeling Positive

Select happily. This may sound unusual, but when anything happens in your life, you have the option of making it a pleasant or terrible experience. Even if it is something negative, you can select what you will learn from it or what you will carry away. Where? Instead of seeking pleasure and positive from outside sources (such as a good career, a great house, or money), look inside (e.g., contentment, pride, intelligence). When? Make happiness and optimism your main priority, and constantly hunt for them. Hold on to tiny pleasant moments, and seek information and skills from the world and people. Find a cause to grin, even if you don't feel it totally, and let that optimism aid with an instant mood boost. Smiling causes your brain to release feel-good chemicals such as dopamine, serotonin, and endorphins. Instead of waiting for anything wonderful to brighten your day, be that positive force for yourself and others. Consider the funniest joke you know. Consider a pleasant recollection. Examine photos or keepsakes that make you happy. Read an encouraging tale. Change your emotional vocabulary. Maintaining a happy attitude may be as simple as changing how you say what you think or feel. Make sure you are not utilizing poor words; instead, determine how you feel and describe it using more detailed emotive phrases. For example, feel "excellent" or "wonderful!" instead of "okay" or "fine!"

Seek expert assistance. If you've tried to cultivate or keep a positive outlook but are still melancholy, miserable, or weeping, it may be time to see a psychologist. Alternatively, speaking with a professional may be beneficial if you are a positive person with a good attitude, but a recent experience has made it harder. Professional mental health experts, such as psychologists or counselors, are qualified to assist you in determining what is going on and achieving your objective of returning to your positive self.

Acting Positive

Negativity should be avoided. If someone taunts you or attempts to hurt you, ignore it or, if you can't ignore it, walk away. Similarly, being in or around pessimism, worry, distrust, or unfavorable judgments might impair your capacity to remain positive. According to life expert Leah Morris, you may avoid certain areas and individuals to retain your optimistic mindset. Suppose you cannot leave a job or other setting. Attempt to keep your interactions as brief as possible. Surround yourself with upbeat individuals. You should surround yourself with positive individuals to retain a happy outlook. Our outlooks, behaviors, and attitudes may influence each other as we spend more time together, so make the time you spend positive. You should also have a positive support system of family and friends to aid you and retain your objective of keeping optimistic. Make a list of the persons with whom you spend the most time. Consider what you see to be their key characteristics. Take note of whether they contribute to or detract from your optimism and how you feel after spending time with them.[74][75]

Engage in active community service. Getting out into the community and performing nice things for others is a terrific approach to acquiring and keeping a cheerful attitude. Helping others gives you a longer-lasting feeling of contentment and positivity. It will also help you observe your great influence on the globe.

Self-care is essential. According to life coach Leah Morris, taking care of oneself is a crucial strategy to boost your happiness. Self-care is essential for maintaining a happy attitude and can encompass everything you intend to properly care for your mental, physical, and emotional health and needs. Allowing yourself time to "recharge your batteries" by exercising self-care is part of being optimistic. Participate in physical self-care. Taking care of your physical self is critical to your body's response to stress and your capacity to maintain a pleasant and healthy mental state. Eating frequently and healthily are two aspects of physical self-care. You are getting adequate sleep and excellent quality sleep. Take care of any medical needs or problems you may have. Ascetic self-care includes activities such as treating oneself with a home spa day

Exercise mental self-care. Just as your physical health can have a detrimental impact on your mental health, your mental health can weaken your immune system and create tiredness and headaches.

---

[74] "10 Tips for Maintaining a Positive Attitude | Indeed.com." 12 Dec. 2019, https://www.indeed.com/career-advice/career-development/how-to-keep-a-positive-attitude.

[75] "Why You Need a Positive Attitude and How to Gain It." https://www.successconsciousness.com/blog/positive-attitude/positive-attitude/.

Practicing meditation can help you maintain your mental self-care. You were using counseling services such as individual treatment: deep breathing exercises, and other relaxing techniques. Visualization is used to imagine oneself as successful.

Maintain your emotional health. Keep your emotional self healthy to recharge your batteries. Take the time to recuperate from any negativity that comes your way and return to a place where you can access the optimism you have worked so hard to achieve. Participating in enjoyable activities may be an example of emotional self-care. For example, you were speaking with someone you haven't seen in a long time. You provided yourself with something to look forward to, such as a vacation. Make a morning habit that you like.

Getting some exercise is one of the simplest ways to boost your mood. It is advised to combat common mental health difficulties such as depression and anxiety, as well as stress from medical illnesses and more significant mental health issues. Exercise has also been demonstrated to release molecules that cause your body to respond positively. Maintaining a cheerful mood may entail incorporating some exercise into your daily routine. Choose a workout and degree of exercise that is appropriate for you. If you don't know of one, consider yoga, which focuses not only on fitness but also on happiness and mindfulness concepts, which are extremely beneficial for a cheerful mood.

How To Change A Negative Attitude

Many studies have found that individuals' reactions to other people and situations are significantly influenced by their viewpoint, not the actual persons or events themselves. Having a negative outlook on life may hurt everyone and everything around you. You may counteract and overcome a negative mindset by actively cultivating optimism.

Letting Go Of Negativity

Accept accountability for your thoughts and behaviors. You alone have authority over your life, and many of the unfavorable events and ideas you have been directly affected by you. By accepting responsibility for your actions, you may begin to eliminate negativity and build positive in your life. Negative ideas generate negative deeds. You will foster beneficial changes if you choose to have an optimistic mindset. For example, it's unlikely that your boss despises you if you don't get a promotion at work because of your work performance. Instead of criticizing your supervisor, discuss with him how you may enhance your job performance and actively implement these improvements. Make a list of the bad aspects of your life and start working on changing them. Recognizing your life's bad aspects can help you realize what you can manage and change. To signify getting rid of negativity, burn the list.

Make a note of everything in your life that you deem bad on a piece of paper. Check off what you can modify as you go through the list. You may alter unfavorable connections with individuals by eliminating them from your life, for example, or you can improve terrible finances by trying to save money. After you've considered how to change the bad influences in your life, burn the paper to represent letting go and make a fresh list of good influences in your life. Expectations must be abandoned. Negativity frequently originates with unrealistic expectations of yourself or others. Allowing yourself to let go of unreasonable or negative expectations will not only help you shift your mindset but will also help you establish a pleasant environment.[76]

Recognize that nothing is flawless. Imperfection adds character and letting go of perfection expectations can let you focus on the positive aspects of any person or circumstance. When something awful occurs, try to forget it as much as possible and then actively visualize what you wish to happen. Similarly, examine it momentarily before dismissing I if someone says anything unfavorable. Dwelling on the bad will only make you feel worse. Finally, forgive yourself as well as others. Holding grudges and concentrating on your flaws will simply highlight your poor attitude. When you can forgive and let go of the negative aspects of yourself and the people you connect with, you can focus on the good.

Forgiveness removes negative attitudes and makes room for good attitudes. However, it will reduce tension and improve serenity and tranquillity in your life. Reduce or eliminate bad individuals from your life. The individuals we associate with have a big influence on our opinions. Limiting or eliminating negative individuals from your life will begin to assist you in changing your mindset. If you can't eliminate someone from your life or don't want to hurt him, you can limit your contact with him. You might also offset his negative attitudes and opinions by emphasizing the good aspects of what he says or does. You won't be dragged down his terrible road this way. Change requires a response. Negative emotions frequently accompany change, and the best approach to deal with change is to

---

[76] "What Is A Positive Attitude and Why Is It Important?." 19 Feb. 2020, https://veteransaffiliatesuccess.com/what-is-a-positive-attitude-and-why-is-it-important/.

adapt rather than react to it. If you decide to respond positively in every scenario, you can keep negativity away.[77]

You can't control everything or everyone, but you can choose how you react to them. Meeting a negative event or person with optimism can maintain your optimistic attitude and may result in a positive conclusion to anything. For example, don't respond immediately if someone writes you a scathing email. Instead, prepare a response and wait 24 hours before sending it. When you return to the email the next day, you will likely tone down your reaction, which can prevent a problem from developing. If you lose your work, thank your boss for the chance and explain that "this is a chance to discover something better that I enjoy." Continue onward. You will occasionally have unpleasant thoughts which are natural and appropriate but learn not to dwell on them. You may transform your bad attitude by continuously going toward the good.

Focusing On The Positive

Look for the good in everything. Negative ideas and attitudes deplete you, and they will become stronger if you give them power. Seeking the good in any person or scenario will assist you in shifting your mentality to a more optimistic one. Even in the worst of circumstances, something positive is always found. It may take some practice, but identifying the good elements of everything can help you avoid negativity. According to one study, a happy attitude correlates to success more than knowledge or abilities. Make a list of everything you're thankful for. Being appreciative will aid in the

---

[77] "15 Tips for Maintaining a Positive Attitude Every Day - Lifehack." 16 Jun. 2022, https://www.lifehack.org/articles/communication/11-tips-for-maintaining-your-positive-attitude.html.

development of a positive mindset. Listing all of the things you're grateful for can help you combat any negative thoughts that may occur.

When you're feeling down, read the list of things you're thankful for. As a sobering reminder, I'll take this to heart. Use positive words. The language you use greatly impacts your attitude and emotional outlook. Using positive phrases and sentiments throughout the day will assist you in being positive and combating negativity. Use statements like "I am optimistic" or "we will find a solution." These will assist you—and others around you—in remaining optimistic. Giving yourself a positive affirmation when you wake up every morning will set the tone for the rest of your day. You may, for example, tell yourself, "Today is going to be an excellent day. I'm in a good mood and eager to make a difference."

Create encouraging quotations and post them in key locations. You will likely have pleasant thoughts and sentiments throughout the day if you surround yourself with good reminders. Surround yourself with upbeat individuals. It is essential to have helped individuals around you who can help you put things into perspective. Surrounding yourself with positive individuals will help you overcome negativity and modify your outlook. Assist others. Simple actions of compassion and service to others can transform your perspective. It may not only put things in perspective in your life, but it can also divert you from issues and make you feel more cheerful. Consider helping out in a hospital or soup kitchen. Knowing you are well and have the resources to sustain yourself can help put your life into perspective. This might also assist you in actively choosing to change negativity in your life. Helping friends and family members can also help you shift a poor attitude since you're making someone else happy, which makes you happy. Giving and receiving love and support will increase your optimistic outlook on life.[78][79][80][81]

[78] "80 Examples of a Positive Attitude - Simplicable." 21 Oct. 2021, https://simplicable.com/en/positive-attitudes.

[79] "Developing a Positive Attitude - Clarke University." https://www.clarke.edu/campus-life/health-wellness/counseling/articles-advice/developing-a-positive-attitude/.

[80] "Positive thinking: Reduce stress by eliminating negative self-talk ...." 03 Feb. 2022, https://www.mayoclinic.org/healthy-lifestyle/stress-management/in-depth/positive-thinking/art-20043950.

[81] "What Is a Positive Attitude? | HealthyPlace." 04 Jul. 2022, https://www.healthyplace.com/self-help/positivity/what-is-a-positive-attitude.

CHAPTER-6

Be Concerned About Other's Needs

Concern for Others is about caring enough — or having the time and energy to care enough — to empathize with others successfully. We've only covered the first four of the Six Essential Aspects of Empathy. Today, we'll look at Concern for Others, which is your ability to care enough about others to display genuine empathy and compassion.

1. **Emotion Contagion:** Before feeling empathy, you must be aware that an emotion is occurring - or that an emotion is required of you. There is much discussion regarding how emotion contagion happens and how we recognize that emotions are expected of us. Still, it is widely acknowledged that the process of empathy is based on our ability to feel and

express emotions. Therefore, empathy is mostly an emotional talent.

2. **Empathic Accuracy** refers to your capacity to recognize and comprehend emotional states and intentions in yourself and others.

3. **Emotion Regulation:** To be a successful empath, you must first learn to comprehend, manage, and deal with your emotions; you must be self-aware. When you recognize and manage your own emotions, you'll be able to perform successfully amid powerful emotions (both yours and others) rather than being overwhelmed or knocked out of commission by them.

4. **Perspective Taking:** This ability allows you to put yourself in the shoes of others creatively, experience circumstances through their eyes, and properly perceive what they may be feeling - allowing you to grasp what others may desire.

5. **Concern for Others:** To have a strong reaction, you must be able to care about the feelings of others and your own. When you experience emotions with others, appropriately recognize those feelings, manage them in yourself, and consider others' perspectives - your sensitive concern will help you interact with others in a way that demonstrates your care and compassion.

6. **Perceptive Engagement:** This ability enables you to make insightful judgments based on empathy and respond or act (if required) in a way that benefits others. Notably, in perceptive engagement, you will frequently do something for someone that would not work for you and may even be

detrimental to your own goals. Perceptive involvement is concerned with the needs of the other person.[82]

These six components of empathy build on each other. Although Emotion Contagion happens intuitively, the others may be cultivated (or calmed down in the case of hyper-empathy) with the empathetic skills you'll learn in The Art of Empathy.

How To Stand Up For Others

If you witness someone being harassed, bullied, or discriminated against, you may recognize that it is wrong but are unclear on how to act and help the victim. Standing up for someone else might be intimidating, and many individuals are hesitant to intervene, but they understand that one voice can make a difference. You can interfere in a scenario by talking to the victim, defusing the situation, and helping the victim after the occurrence. You may also avoid bullying and harassment at your school or community.

Preventing Bullying And Harassment

Stop having unpleasant talks. Put an end to any talks that are derogatory or gossipy about others. Even if you don't like the person being trashed, it's important to warn the trash-talker not to speak adversely about others. Even if you don't know the person you're destroying, you can still help. You can defend the individual who is being trashed. For instance, if someone says, "Maddie irritates me! "She's so unattractive," you may respond, "That's nasty. That's not

---

[82] "What is Positive Mental Attitude? 9 ways to inculcate it.." https://www.proudhr.com/what-is-positive-mental-attitude/.

how you talk about people. Maddie is attractive, in my opinion." Tell the speaker to stop referring to other individuals in this manner. You can remark, "I don't believe it's appropriate to mock him this way. Please halt." If they persist, leave the discussion. Something else in the bully's life might be causing them to bully others. People may behave out when stressed or having other problems at home. They may have either been bullied themselves or been a victim of abuse. These folks may require further assistance, such as mental health therapy, to address these concerns. Make an effort to enquire about these options politely. Please encourage them to get help from a skilled expert by providing helpful counsel.

Be an anti-bullying activist. Teach others how to confront bullies and advocate for what is right. Find materials on anti-bullying or anti-discrimination that are appropriate for your audience, educate yourself, and share what you've learned. Look for materials that promote a cause you believe in and are useful to your audience. For example, you could want to learn about bullying to increase awareness at your high school, or you might want to learn about hate crimes against minorities to raise awareness in your community. People will be more open to your campaign if it is something they can relate to. Assist your local community, business, or schools in developing a reporting system so that victims may get aid more easily. Communities, companies, and schools may use these methods to help establish simple and practical ways for victims to report bullying or harassment. They can also use these data to track bullying and harassment patterns over time to build better preventative strategies.

If you are a student, you may create an anti-bullying organization or talk to your school's administration about what you can do to prevent bullying at your school. Take steps to combat cyberbullying. If you're online and notice someone making disparaging remarks about someone or sending abusive messages to them, report their account. Most social networking networks allow you to report users for abusive conduct, and practically every website's Terms of Service define cyberbullying as abusive behavior. Remind individuals to pause before posting. Once you submit something, it is no longer under your control and will remain perpetually on the internet. For example, if your friend posts anything derogatory about a classmate, you may respond, "Do you want to put that on the internet? It may easily come back to him and make you seem awful."[83]

Treat them on the internet the same way you treat them in person. Avoid saying anything if you don't have anything nice to say, or express your disagreement politely if you do. Avoid utilizing websites that allow you to remain anonymous. People occasionally use anonymity features on websites to harass others. Allow your parents to access your passwords and social media accounts if you are a child or adolescent. They can assist you if you have any internet troubles. Talk to folks who are not like you. Attempt to learn more about individuals different from you regarding ethnicity, culture, religion, or sexual orientation. A better understanding of a person's life increases your empathy for them and their situation. Encourage a culture of empathy in the people in your life. Knowing more about another person's narrative can aid in the prevention of bullying and encourage others to speak out against it. Make friends with peers or coworkers from other backgrounds. As you get to know

---

[83] "21 Ways to Create and Maintain a Positive Attitude." https://daringtolivefully.com/positive-attitude.

someone more, you may discover that you have a lot in common—volunteer for a cause that helps others in different situations than you. For example, you may volunteer at a homeless shelter, provide housing for a refugee family, or collaborate with your faith community to establish a fellowship with a different religious group. Read books about or written by someone from a different background than your own.

Speaking Up For Someone Else

Be confident. Don't wait for a victim of bullying to come out and seek your assistance. They could feel too threatened to say anything. Take command of the issue and stand out for the other person first; they could be relieved that they don't have to. Recognize that victims in an aggressive scenario may be in a physiological "freeze" trauma response, which is a frequent reaction to high stress. They may be frozen by fear and unable to reply properly, necessitating the intervention of a bystander. You are not alone if you find it difficult to speak up. Many people find it difficult. However, when one individual speaks up, others are likely to follow suit. Because of a genuine or apparent relationship with the bully, you may be able to assist in de-escalate some situations. If you share the bully's race, gender, or culture, the bully may be more willing to listen to you because they believe they have something in common with you. Knowing the bully may make you more likely to intervene successfully because you can hold them accountable.

Break up the harassing. When you notice the bully tormenting the victim, ignore the aggressor and walk straight to the victim. Before you intervene, thoroughly examine the situation for safety. If you feel safe, you can physically come in between the victim and the bully to talk to the victim. Make every effort to separate the victim from the bully as soon as feasible. Otherwise, approach the sufferer as closely as possible. You begin the dialogue with the victim, allowing them to determine whether or not they should interfere. As you examine the scenario, search for any potential weapons. Determine whether the offender is making physical threats, whether the victim has been wounded, and whether this is a case of sexual harassment or abuse. Contact the local police and emergency medical services immediately if these things happen.[84][85]

You can do this whether or not you know the individual. To cease the harassment, the victim will most likely be willing to cooperate. You may remark, "Hey, I've been hunting for you everywhere!" or "Oh my god, how are you?" When dealing with the bully, exercise care. In many circumstances, confronting the bully directly may not be the best approach, especially if you are afraid they would physically abuse you. You might become the bully's next victim. While keeping a safe distance, making direct eye contact with the bully is prudent. Take decisive action. You can do this without confronting the bully. This will help you establish control of the situation as you cautiously approach the victim. Using this method will also provide a comprehensive description of the bully in case you need to report the event to law enforcement later. However, if you are satisfied that the issue will not develop and that you will not become a target, you may approach the bully. Bullies frequently want to be popular and strong, and calling them out may help reduce their power. You may intervene and say, "Please leave him

---

[84] "The Power of a Positive Attitude - NAHCA | The CNA Association." 20 Mar. 2022, https://www.nahcacna.org/the-power-of-a-positive-attitude/.

[85] "10 Ways To Have a More Positive Attitude at Work | Indeed.com." 12 Dec. 2019, https://www.indeed.com/career-advice/career-development/positive-attitude-at-work.

alone! Take a step back right now!" Be forceful, vocal, and firm in your stance. You may not feel brave but act as if you do. When interfering, seek assistance. Identify a person of influence who can help you resolve the problem. This may be a supervisor, police enforcement, or someone with more authority than you who is better suited to tackle the situation.

As soon as you feel the situation is risky, dial 911 or your local emergency number. Inform an adult. If you are a youngster or adolescent, locate an adult you can trust to assist you in dealing with someone else who is being bullied or mistreated. Adults may frequently use their power to deal with the problem without the bully knowing what happened. If you cannot identify someone in a position of authority to assist you, collect additional witnesses to assist you in intervening and stopping the bullying. There is power in numbers. Inform others about any continued bullying or harassment. Speak out if you see bullying, harassment, or prejudice. Tell someone, even if it did not affect you or you were not present at the time, and raise awareness. Not saying anything will exacerbate the situation for everyone. Inform someone in authority about the harassment or bullying you are seeing. Telling your teacher about someone being bullied in an area of the school where there is limited monitoring can be done in several ways. If you see harassment in the workplace breakroom, notify your supervisor or HR representative so that another witness can be present.

You can do so anonymously if you are too shy to speak up in person. Some organizations offer options to report employee misconduct anonymously ("whistleblowing"), schools may have ways to report trouble anonymously, and many localities have tip lines where people may contact police enforcement anonymously. You are not alone if you find it difficult to speak up. Many people find it difficult. However, when one individual stands up, more and more people follow suit. Sometimes it only takes one individual to point out an injustice before many people feel strong enough to speak up.

Supporting A Victim

Assist the victim in standing up to the bully. A victim of bullying may wish to confront the bully but does not know how or is frightened to do it on their own. Offer your support and ask if they want you to assist them in standing up to the bully. Inquire about how you may assist them in standing up to their harasser. For example, "Would you want to meet me after class so we can face her together before lunch?" you may offer. Or "If you wish, I may accompany you to the meeting with the supervisor. I will stand by you and bear testimony." Don't be surprised if they say no.

Some people dislike relying on another person's assistance to stop bullying. If they tell you no, you could say, "Okay, but if you change your mind, I'll help you," and stick to it! Pay attention to the victim. The victim should be believed, and their tale should be listened to if they come to you for aid. Find out how you may assist them if they require it. It is critical to trust the victim even if you did not see the occurrence. As they talk, be nonjudgmental and encouraging. Doubting their tale may make them feel even more violated and isolated. As they tell their experience, listen with empathy. You could remark, "What happened to you seems dreadful. You appear to be disturbed. What can I do to assist you?"[86][87]

Assist the sufferer in obtaining assistance. Because the victim may be too disturbed to seek out useful resources on their own, take the initiative and offer to discover some for them. Offer your aid in whatever way you feel comfortable doing so. Is someone being harassed on the street? You may help them safely get back to their house. You might call the police on the victim's behalf and accompany them when they submit a police complaint. Provide your contact information to the victim and the police so that you may be a witness in any legal procedures. You might assist the victim in connecting with any legal assistance or anti-bullying services they may require.

Allow the victim to feel upset. The victim will probably vent their frustrations on you after the occurrence. Take nothing personally. The victim may believe you are a "safe" person to vent their frustrations to. The victim may reply something along the lines of, "I'm sorry you got involved. I can look after myself!" You may say something like, "I apologize. From my vantage point, the scenario appeared to be harassment. Unless you want it, I will not meddle again." The sufferer may weep, become angry, or experience shock. It's OK to sit with them and simply be there; you don't need to come up with some magic words to say.

---

[86] "5 Ways to Build a Positive Attitude - wikiHow." 17 Mar. 2022, https://www.wikihow.com/Build-a-Positive-Attitude.

[87] "100+ Positive Attitude Quotes for Life - The STRIVE." 18 Nov. 2021, https://thestrive.co/positive-attitude-quotes/.

How To Be Tolerant Of Others

You may be unable to put up with someone's actions or words. Avoid turning it into a personal battle by attempting to understand where each person is coming from. Instead, you might strive to cultivate a more tolerant viewpoint by learning about diverse individuals, growing self-confidence, and learning to embrace difference.

Tolerating Others In Difficult Situations

Attempt to empathize. Making a deliberate effort to sympathize with and understand things from his point of view is a smart first step in tolerating people in difficult circumstances. Because you may come from diverse backgrounds and experiences, what is apparent to you may appear bizarre or foreign to someone else. Request an explanation. If you're talking to someone and they say something you find difficult to accept, you can figure out their point of view without becoming intolerant or hostile. Request that someone clarifies their point of view to you to better grasp it. You may say, for example, "Okay, please elaborate. What makes you believe that?"

You are being tolerant by not dismissing them outright, seeking to grasp something that you find difficult to accept. Tolerance does not imply accepting undesirable conduct. Ignore your disagreements. One approach to dealing with a tough circumstance is to disregard your disagreements. This is a more negative form of tolerance than learning to embrace and cherish diversity, yet it may be beneficial. To do this, you must avoid specific subjects of conversation or quickly shift the subject when required. Use "I" statements instead of "you" ones. It might be beneficial to avoid making allegations or assumptions about the person you are conversing with. You may utilize "I" statements rather than "you" ones. This can help de-escalate any personal enmity and make you more open to each other's points of view. For example, if you're talking about schools providing contraception to teens, you may say, "I think it's reasonable for schools to provide contraception." This is a considerate way of expressing yourself. Avoid using "you" in phrases such as "You're dumb for thinking that schools shouldn't provide contraception."

Resolve a disagreement. If you cannot sympathize with or ignore the situation and find it difficult to endure, you might try to confront it to seek a resolution. If you are excellent friends with someone and don't want this intolerance to de-rail your connection, it's worth trying to find a solution together. Everyone participating must be willing to put up an effort and contribute completely. Begin by quietly stating what you find insulting or unbearable in each other's conduct or perspectives. "I disagree with your view on gun control," for example. You'll then need to understand each other's cultural perspectives better. You may ask, "What experiences prompted you to establish your beliefs concerning gun control?" Then, describe how the matter would be handled in each other's culture or point of view. You may begin by articulating your ideal circumstance and enable the other person to do the same. For example, you may begin by saying, "I believe we should make it more difficult to get weapons because..." Then you may start negotiating a path forward that considers and respects your differences. This will be simpler if you misunderstand each other's actions rather than if you hold more or less opposing viewpoints. For instance, you may begin by saying, "While I disagree with your points of view, I now have a greater understanding of them. Now that I know why you believe what you believe, I can better appreciate your point of view and am ready to go on."

Developing A More Tolerant Outlook

The difference in value. Understanding and valuing differences are important to creating a more tolerant mindset. People who embrace diversity and uniqueness are more tolerant of others and less agitated by ambiguity and uncertainty. Because it overlooks the variety and complexity, intolerance may efficiently narrow down and simplify an ever-changing environment, making it simpler to grasp. Adopting a more open-minded attitude and exposing yourself to different points of view and cultures can help you become more tolerant. Talk to strangers and read publications or websites you wouldn't ordinarily look at. Interact with individuals of all ages and cultures.[88][89]

Accept the unknown. According to research, ambiguity intolerance or the inability to handle uncertainty are fundamental personality qualities of persons who are less tolerant of others. National research has found that nations with individuals who are more forgiving of uncertainty are more accepting of dissent, tolerant of deviance, less risk-averse, and more favorable toward young people. You might strive to be more accepting of ambiguity by focusing on answers rather than questions. The concept is that if you are continually looking for a solution, you will believe that there is only one answer and that response is constant and unchanging. There are frequently several solutions to the same topic, and by being open-minded and

---

[88] "Top 7 Benefits Of A Positive Attitude - The STRIVE." 13 Dec. 2021, https://thestrive.co/benefits-of-a-positive-attitude/.
[89] "18 Simple Ways to Keep a Positive Attitude at Work." https://wheniwork.com/blog/18-simple-ways-to-keep-a-positive-attitude-at-work.

inquiring, you will become more conscious of the variances and more forgiving of the ambiguity. Learn about various cultures and people. Becoming more welcoming may be achieved by becoming more educated about the other cultures around you. When people lack tolerance for someone, it is often due to a sense of alienation about what the other person is saying. Spend some time learning about diverse civilizations and belief systems. Do not be scared to ask questions, but do so respectfully and politely.

For example, you may learn about various ways to commemorate key events. You may also expose yourself to fresh experiences to help you understand topics that previously appeared foreign or alien to you. Examine your sentiments of intolerance. Understanding the context and origins of your intolerant sentiments may assist you in recognizing and challenging them. Consider why you've been critical of others in the past. Were you raised to believe that certain individuals are better than you, or have you experienced terrible experiences? Determine why you feel a specific way about a particular set of individuals. For example, perhaps you were up in a family where insulting remarks against persons of a specific race or religion were widespread. Perhaps you had an unpleasant experience with someone of a different race or religion, and that event contributed to your perceptions about that individual. Improve your self-esteem. People who are unhappy with themselves or have poor or negative self-esteem are more prone to be intolerant of others. This intolerance may be a reflection of how someone perceives himself. If you feel more safe and confident, you may discover you are more open-minded and tolerant of other people. Consider a challenging notion. Practicing coping with ideas that you find uncomfortable is an intriguing method to attempt to become more tolerant. This is an approach used by psychologists and can be an effective way to manage intolerance. It operates on the premise that it is tough to retain difficult thinking and that attempting so can help you learn to deal with unpleasant situations.

We tend to avoid or escape from challenging thoughts, which can lead to an irritable, impatient, or unsympathetic attitude. Instead, choose a tough thought and ponder it for at least 10 seconds daily. For example, suppose you find the prospect of abandoning your faith unacceptable. In that case, you may decide, "I am going to renounce my religion and become a Buddhist (or another religion that is not your own)." Then consider what occurs next. Do you have an emotional reaction? What are the following ideas that spring to mind?

How To Be Happy For Others

It might be tough at times to be pleased for others, but eliminating envious impulses can bring substantial benefits to your work or social life and your mental well-being. You may relieve the tension and worry you feel when others succeed by concentrating on what you're grateful for and why it's beneficial for you and them that you share in their happiness.

Changing Your Attitude To Be Positive

Change your mentality by using positive affirmations. Positive affirmations are simply the practice of repeating a positive remark to oneself regularly to alter your view and perspective. This technique can help lessen tension and defensiveness in response to threats to our sense of self. Every time you are presented with a difficult situation, repeat a simple remark about being pleased for others. In your positive affirmations, use declarative sentences. For example,

"I can be glad for others and respect their hard work," or "I am pleased for my friends and family because I want them to be happy as well." Allow yourself to be competitive when there is no reason to be. It may be tiring to feel the urge to compete with individuals close to you. It's difficult enough to live a happy life without seeing the victories of others as losses for you. Strive to appreciate their accomplishments, and you will avoid the tension and frustration of viewing their victories incorrectly.[90][91]

A win for others is not a defeat for you. Participate in their successes, and they will learn to participate in yours. Use the successes of others as motivation for your own. Consider whether you want to be happy. Feeling envious of others may be incredibly unpleasant and is frequently unnecessary. We choose to be unhappy by hanging on to a bad frame of mind, such as envy. Rather, opt to isolate yourself from bad feelings. Push out bad emotions by focusing on good ones like negative ideas. The decision to be joyful is symbolic, but the commitment to changing your thinking must be genuine. Make their triumph your own. It's tempting to regard other people's accomplishments as competing with your own; instead, examine how they are also yours. Allow yourself the chance to make it all about you (inside your head).

Consider how you assisted a friend or coworker in the recent or distant past. Consider when you answered questions, listened carefully, or said something encouraging. You put money into their success and can now partake in it. Nobody will succeed just to spite

---

[90] "Positive Thinking: Definition, Benefits, and How to Practice." 25 Feb. 2011, https://www.verywellmind.com/what-is-positive-thinking-2794772.

[91] "Positive thinking: Reduce stress by eliminating negative self-talk ...." 03 Feb. 2022, https://www.mayoclinic.org/healthy-lifestyle/stress-management/in-depth/positive-thinking/art-20043950.

you. Everyone is on their path, and for most of us, each trip is filled with highs and lows. When someone achieves a high point, don't think it has anything to do with you; rather, consider it a part of the trip they began long ago. Remember that the achievement of others is neither personal nor directed at you. Remove yourself from the equation and reconsider the matter. You most likely have minimal influence over the person's motivations.

Using Your Actions To Shift Your Thinking

Exude happiness. When you allow jealousy to cloud your judgment, it can be difficult to be happy for others. Instead, concentrate on being optimistic. Even if your friends' success underwhelms you, remember that their achievement means something to them. Being supportive of your friends when they accomplish you will assist in developing a supportive connection that will benefit you both. Positive thinking can help you feel better. It is wonderful to share in the happiness of others, and you could realize that the joyful sensation alone is worth the effort. If you find it difficult to overcome feelings of envy when you watch others achieve, it might be because you are underestimating your accomplishments, triumphs, or things in your thoughts. Make a list of everything for which you should be thankful. Review the list regularly and add to it as needed. Consider your list whenever you are tempted to be envious of someone else. You may have decided to be happy for other people, but it doesn't change how you feel. Instead, regulate your outer look to convey your joy for others.[92]

---

[92] "What is positive thinking? 6 ways to use the power of positive thinking." https://www.tonyrobbins.com/positive-thinking/.

It's good to say something pleasant inadvertently; the gesture is still valuable. You may discover that you love the act of applauding others' successes, making the step to real appreciation simpler. Share in the joy of others. Allowing others' happiness to make you happy can help you create great relationships. Relationships evolve or alter based on how you engage with one another, and displaying your enjoyment for others increases the likelihood that those individuals will advocate on your behalf in the future. Sharing in the joy of others is an excellent method to make new friends and build solid professional ties. Making a good impression on people may help you both socially and professionally.[93]

Using Positivity In Conversation

When speaking, just employ good words and push away negative ideas. You will find it much simpler to be glad for others if you learn to regulate how you talk and think. Avoid focusing on the negative parts of anything while positively managing your discourse. Don't let negative ideas consume you; concentrate on the good. Controlling your concentration will become simpler with experience.

Choose to say good things to your coworkers and friends to put yourself in a better mood and show appreciation for them. Compliment someone directly. You don't have to be extremely inventive in expressing your joy for others. Try just complimenting them on the effort they've made or the predicament they've found themselves in. When feasible, give them the compliment in person. Maintain simplicity. You share the attention and establish yourself

---

[93] "Positive Thinking: What It Is and How to Do It - WebMD."
https://www.webmd.com/mental-health/positive-thinking-overview.

as a team player by shining the focus on the accomplishments of others. The individuals you mention will likely appreciate the act, which will deepen your relationship with them and encourage others to do the same.

How to Be a More Friendly Person

It has been established that having close relatives and friends who can function as your support system can make you healthier and happier. Unfortunately, it's not always easy to keep friends or relatives around, especially if you're harsh to them or have a persistent bad attitude about them. Fortunately, this does not have to remain the case indefinitely. You may become under and establish meaningful relationships with people if you practice kindness regularly and learn to control your anger.

Controlling Your Anger

Relaxation practices might help you calm down. Take a moment to calm yourself as soon as you recognize you are becoming irritated. One effective method is to use a relaxing technique. Among the alternatives are:

- Deep breathing.
- Listening to soothing music.
- Progressive muscle relaxation.
- Meditation.
- Take a walk.
- Listening to a podcast.

Refute unrealistic assertions or ideas. Unrealistic thinking patterns can amplify emotions of rage, so try to recognize and address them as they arise. For instance, an unrealistic idea may be, "My roommate never contributes to keeping our apartment tidy! Everything is done by myself!" Before you allow yourself to become furious due to this idea, consider whether it is true. Does your roommate do anything different than you to keep the flat clean? If this is the case, the term "never" in this sentence is unrealistic. Try rephrasing the thinking or remark, "I wish my roommate would chip in a bit more than she does with domestic tasks." Enhance your problem-solving abilities. Good problem-solving abilities can also aid in the reduction of feelings of rage and irritation. Even if you are dealing with something upsetting, it may help you feel more in control. This is a talent that takes time to master, so be patient.

When faced with an issue, try to recognize it before attempting to fix it. Then, compile a list of the alternative options and select the best one. After implementing your solution, evaluate how it went and consider how you may improve your plan in the future. Don't let your resentment or anger fester. Keeping your anger within is not a good idea when you can't say anything and are irritated. Instead of allowing your aggravation to escalate into wrath, speak up and tackle the cause of your annoyance. Don't be scared to make an unpleasant moment awkward since talking it out is preferable to being cruel in the future.

If you've been mistreated or injured by someone, you might desire to cause them the same emotional agony. Instead, let them know that their actions damaged your feelings and made you feel disrespectful. Instead of letting your rage fester, tell the offender what they did wrong. Say anything like this: "That is not something

I approve of. It irritates and angers me greatly." Next, put your efforts into something productive. Instead of being rude to others, channel your energy into a sport or pastime you like. Finally, maintain your level of activity. When you exercise or do anything active, your brain releases endorphins that make you happy.[94][95]

You can participate in a team sport such as football, baseball, soccer, or hockey. If you don't enjoy physical activities, consider something artistic, such as learning to play an instrument or painting. When you become irritated, go away. Recognize when your anger begins to boil over and be aware of how angry you are. Be courteous and explain why you're leaving. However, don't leave the situation hanging indefinitely. When your wrath dissipates, regain your composure and speak to the individual again.

Being Kind To Others

Experiment with becoming more compassionate. Try to be more personable and tolerant of others' viewpoints. Instead of making sarcastic remarks, think of ways you may make someone's day better. Do something nice for someone every day; they'll appreciate it. Paying someone praise instead of making fun of them to lift your spirits can make them feel better and improve their day. Practicing compassion may make you a healthier and happier person. You may also show appreciation for a buddy by purchasing a modest present such as candies or a book. Improve your communication abilities. The ability to listen effectively and speak in a constructive, forceful manner may also assist you in feeling in control of your anger and

---

[94] "What is Positive Thinking in Psychology? 9 Thought-Provoking Findings." 13 Aug. 2021, https://positivepsychology.com/positive-thinking/.
[95] "Positive Thinking | SkillsYouNeed." https://www.skillsyouneed.com/ps/positive-thinking.html.

being compassionate to others. Communicating your sentiments and emotions can assist others in comprehending your state of mind and alleviate a great deal of tension. Arguments or disputes sometimes emerge due to a lack of communication and understanding of people's intentions. Try to be more honest in the discussion, even if it makes the scenario less than ideal or you believe the individual would dislike you for it. Do not avoid discussing subjects that make you uncomfortable.

Remove all distractions and offer the person your undivided attention. Try to keep your judgment at bay while you listen. Simply attempt to comprehend what the other person is saying and where they are coming from. When expressing oneself, utilize "I" statements rather than "you" phrases. For example, try saying, "I get annoyed when you fail to clean up your dishes." On the other hand, saying "You never pick up after yourself!" is inappropriate.

Communicating successfully sometimes entails being vulnerable and discussing potentially uncomfortable topics. It's better to say, "It made me sad when you made that joke, and everyone laughed, and I'm sorry for making you laugh at the expense of your feelings." I felt humiliated, and while you didn't think it was a big thing, it greatly wounded my feelings." Be a little more patient. People cannot read your mind, and some take longer than others to learn new things. Instead of being enraged right away, be more patient with them. Consider a period when you were learning something new or needed assistance. Recognize that no one is flawless. Instead of letting anything irritate you until you become furious, address the individual and talk.[96]

If your roommate is tapping their pencil, interfering with your work, say something like, "Hey, I know it seems strange, but I can't finish this paper while you're tapping that pencil. Do you mind if I come to a halt while I finish my work?" Don't be jaded. Being cynical all of the time might make you unhappy and angry. Cynicism is typically a protective strategy when you are dissatisfied or feel let down. Instead of expressing your emotions healthy and useful, you bottle them up and minimize their influence on others and yourself. This can lead to a pessimistic outlook on the world and a continual feeling of rage.

Don't disparage other people's labor or efforts. When someone excels at something, admire them instead of ignoring or downplaying it. Reduce the amount of judgment you pass on to others. If you don't comprehend a group of individuals, strive to learn about them rather than despise them. Empathy should be practiced. Understanding and internalizing another person's experiences and emotions are what empathy entails. Put yourself in the shoes of the other person and talk to them without placing judgment on them first. When someone is in agony, relate to them instead of discounting their emotions. Internalize what they're saying and strive to feel their feelings. This might help you better grasp their point of view and actions.

Concentrate on paying attention to what the individual is saying, offer feedback to demonstrate that you're listening, and delay any

---

[96] "Think Positive: 11 Ways to Boost Positive Thinking." 06 Mar. 2018, https://www.psychologytoday.com/us/blog/click-here-happiness/201803/think-positive-11-ways-boost-positive-thinking.

judgment you may have. Instead of condemning them, attempt to encourage them. Consider a period when you were in a similar situation and try to remember how horrible it felt. Stop defending yourself. Don't put up barriers and be wary of everyone you encounter.—this harm your relations with others. If you've done anything wrong, accept personal responsibility for your actions and don't place blame on others. Be open to creating new acquaintances and strengthening current ones. Instead of becoming enraged at someone for pointing out a flaw, say something like, "You are correct. I'm working on it, but it will take some time." Instead of quickly dismissing unfavorable comments, ask the individual, "What do you mean by that?" After clarifying, it may not be as dangerous as you first imagined.

Doing Selfless Acts

When you notice someone in need, assist them. Rather than turning away or assuming that it is someone else's job, do your best to assist those in need. Think of easy activities you can do during your day to aid folks who can't help themselves. For example, you may assist a younger family member in setting up their computer or an older person in carrying their groceries. The more you serve people on your initiative, the happier you will be. Make additional efforts around the house. If you're younger, this involves performing your tasks without being asked and attempting to assist your family when you notice they're stressed. Fixing a damaged item and making dinner for your partner are simple ways to show that you care about your loved ones. Find other activities around the house to relieve your partner's tension. Communicate with your family and ask if they need anything else done around the house. A clean and orderly home might genuinely increase your energy and happiness. When your friends need someone to talk to, be there for them. Friendship is an important factor in your pleasure. Having a support system to turn to in difficult times offers us a sense of belonging. Having friends lowers your blood pressure and makes you less susceptible to depression. Friendship, on the other hand, is formed through communication and vulnerability. Friends will avoid you if you are nasty or judgmental, and they will be less supportive when you need them.

Maintain your focus and listen. Friends don't always want advice; they just want someone to speak to. If you've talked to a buddy about a severe issue, it'll be simpler to talk to them about serious concerns in your life. Make an effort to better your neighborhood. Other local projects should be investigated, such as efforts to plant trees or beautify your neighborhood. You'll be happier and less prone to lash out if you get to know other people working hard for a better future. As a result, you'll be happier and less angry if you participate in volunteer work with a group of others. Finally, having a support system when things are challenging might help us cope with daily stress.[97][98]

---

[97] "Power Of Positive Thinking: 7 Mindful Habits For Positivity." https://thelawofattraction.com/power-of-positive-thinking/.

[98] "The Power of Positive Thinking: 6 Ways to Be Happy All Day Long." 16 Jan. 2019, https://blog.mindvalley.com/the-power-of-positive-thinking/.

CHAPTER-7

Be Approachable

What goes around comes around - and it truly does with love. According to research, being kind to others boosts both our own and their happiness. Furthermore, because kindness is contagious, it makes our communities a better place to live. Recent brain research has revealed that people are hard-wired for love and compassion. So it's not just about individual achievement - our communities and society grow when people look out for one other. When we are nice to others, we know that it improves our bonds with them and gives us a source of support. According to research, we may benefit more from assisting than from getting it - and we are also more likely to receive it in return when we need it. This may not be like-for-like assistance or even from the same person, but being nice to others fosters a larger support network, increasing overall well-being.

Doing good for strangers fosters cooperation, trust, and a sense of safety in our communities. It also allows us to perceive others more favorably and empathize with them. These are the pillars of a successful local community and a flourishing society, which promotes overall well-being. Kindness might be as simple as a smile, a thank you, or an encouraging phrase. It's a way of connecting with individuals we pass in our everyday lives, even if only for a little minute. It doesn't have to be time-consuming; what matters is that it is an act of real concern and attention for another person. There are other suggestions below and across this page. Kind deeds can be spontaneous, such as when we discover someone in need. For example, we may give up our train seats or pick up and return someone's dropped glove. Opportunities to be nice abound, such as passing on a newspaper we've done reading, allowing someone to use our parking space, or passing on an unused ticket. Kind deeds can also be planned, such as doing something for a friend, neighbor, or loved one or spreading some everyday joy. There are infinite ways to be nice to others; we must keep our eyes open and pay attention to individuals around us to begin noticing possibilities to assist. To be kind, we must be aware of the people around us and pay attention to their needs and feelings. We all have underlying compassion, but it might take some time for us to recognize it.[99]

Researchers discovered that when people remembered assisting others, they felt a surge of euphoria. According to research, the "helper's high" is more than just a mood, as biochemical examination found favorable improvements in the body's

---

[99] "Positive Thinking Quotes (3487 quotes) - Goodreads."
https://www.goodreads.com/quotes/tag/positive-thinking.

immunological functioning and reduced levels of stress chemicals.[100]

When someone acts kindly, the mesolimbic pathway in the brain is refreshed and stimulated, reinforcing stimuli and releasing "feel-good" neurotransmitters like vasopressin and oxytocin. As a result, acts of generosity provide a cheerful, gratifying, and tranquil sensation on the inside, and the individual is more willing to repeat these connected behaviors. Scientific study has shown that the same brain region is stimulated while donating to charity, which gives us the joy of fulfillment while eating. Another study discovered that helping others begins in the same place of the brain as enjoying the delight of the reward. People's preexisting moral views substantially influence their generosity. In the light of facts, it seems that donating is always accompanied by compassion and sympathy, emotions associated with moral behavior.

Beneficient action looks to be an excellent technique for personal satisfaction. You have a specific objective while giving works best for the giver. This impact is not limited to the objective of making someone joyful. Instead, it is associated with spiritual joy, self-satisfaction, and a closer relationship with your creator. It makes little difference if the aim is intended to help an individual, a group, or society; a clear plan exceeds an abstract purpose and brings immense delight to the provider. A clear objective is more satisfying than a dispersed aim because it provides more realistic chances of accomplishment. A particular goal helps one foresee changes and

---

[100] "What Is Positive Thinking and How to Always Think Positive." https://www.lifehack.org/875426/positive-thinking.

obstacles more effectively, allowing one more confidence in doing something good for the world rather than merely wishing it were so.

How To Be More Approachable

Simple modifications in body language can make you appear more accessible, particularly when attempting to gain the attention of strangers or acquaintances. If you display humility, trustworthiness, and confidence, those who already know you will approach you for more serious talk. Adjusting your behavior this way might be difficult, but the effort is well worth the deeper, more successful connections.

Using Approachable Body Language

Take an open stance. Instead of sagging forward, keep your head high and your shoulders straight. Lean back somewhat and put yourself at ease while sitting. Instead of being walled off and unwelcoming, this stance exposes your face proudly to the world. Keep your arms in a friendly stance. Position your arms at your sides or on your lap. Keep your hands to the side or towards your lower torso while holding anything or making motions. Avoid awkward poses, such as crossed arms or hands in front of your chest. Although psychology studies are mixed on this topic, enthusiastic postures with hands lifted over your head may make you more difficult to approach. Simply smiling makes you appear more personable and inviting. A forced or artificial grin, on the other hand, is not nearly as effective. Consider a good recollection or a hilarious joke to bring a real grin to your face. Smiling can also help you feel happier.

Make direct eye contact. People are significantly more inclined to approach someone who looks them in the eyes than someone who turns away or avoids their sight. A smile and prolonged eye contact may make all the difference. There are a few alternatives for women to choose from to liven things up: A bold flirt involves making eye contact with the person in question for only a few seconds, smiling, and then shifting your eyes to something else. To appear adorable and coy, establish brief eye contact with someone gazing in your way, then glance down or in another direction and grin.

Looking More Approachable Through Other Methods

Items that impede your view should be avoided. Sunglasses, hats, and scarves may all obscure your face. Even if they aren't immediately blocking your vision, the psychological effect may make you appear more secluded and harder to approach. Place distracting stuff on the floor. You could miss out on looks, smiles, and other indications that could lead to a dialogue. Develop your physical look. It may appear superficial, but those who put care into their looks may appear more inviting. Consider straightening your clothing, dressing appropriately, or perhaps getting a makeover. Try the "peacocking" technique. Wear accessories that stick out, such as distinctive rings or belts, so that others notice and comment on them. They are excellent discussion starters. Take care of your hygiene. Regularly wash your body and hair, clean your teeth, and keep your nails clipped. Wear clean clothes and clear up any mold in your home that may contribute to a persistent, unpleasant odor in clothing or accessories.

Approaching Others And Building Relationships

Take an interest in other people. When conversing with another individual, ask questions about his life and attempt to spend more time listening than talking. Make this a habit to establish yourself as a sympathetic, friendly person. Learn to watch people if you have problems picking up on social signs. Improve your social skills to engage more successfully with others, and practice empathizing with their worries and points of view. Experiment with "drive-by compliments." These are delightful, heartwarming gifts for those in your life. As you go by, compliment someone on their looks, recent acts, or personality. You can improve her attitude, establish yourself as a kind person, and possibly even start a praising trend.[101][102]

Make a list of discussion starters. Being personable is only half the fight when meeting new people. You'll have to persuade them to stay as well. Prepare discussion ideas to discuss before attending an event. Make sure to include a "popular" topic, such as a recent movie or piece of sports news, so you are more likely to meet someone who shares that interest. To get a more in-depth response, use open-ended questions instead of just "yes" or "no." Make your talks relevant to the event or place you're at. If most of the audience is students, you can discuss recent campus news or an intellectual issue. You can discuss the band, person, or art you've all gathered to see at concerts and many other events. Finally, prepare responses to frequently asked questions. "How's it going?" someone inquires. "Fine," you say. That dialogue, on the other hand, did not go anywhere. Prepare for typical queries like this by telling the other person about something fascinating that has happened in your life. Instead of uneasy quiet, this can lead to a real dialogue.

---

[101] "The Power of Positive Thinking | Benefits of Positive Thinking." 23 Jan. 2016, https://www.jonathanparker.org/mind-power/the-power-of-positive-thinking/.

[102] "What Is Positive Thinking and Why You Need It." https://www.successconsciousness.com/blog/positive-attitude/what-is-positive-thinking/.

Understand how to deal with cultural prejudices. Stereotypes, workplace politics, and even fashion preferences might discourage someone from approaching you. —Try to learn about a new town's, workplace's, or other community's manners. Many prejudices, such as those based on gender, age, or race, are unavoidable. Recognize, however, that many knee-jerk reactions are based on "implicit bias," which refers to an unconscious and automatic reaction that may not reflect the other person's views. As a result, you may observe a drastically different reaction if you attempt to initiate a discussion or create a connection.

Avoid snide remarks and gossip. Even if made in jest, mean statements can irritate people and make you appear unpleasant and ungenerous. Avoid gossip as well, as it might get you a reputation for spreading secrets or operating behind people's backs. Try to stay away from themes like politics and religion. Instead, attempt to include others in discussions. Make room in a conversation for a newcomer, introduce him, or ask his name. If he appears perplexed, let someone in on an inside joke. Don't assume that someone wants to be alone because he doesn't participate in discussions or attend social activities. Make an effort to approach individuals, and you can find yourself with more and stronger friendships. When you discover a secret, take it seriously. Demonstrate to others that they can rely on you. People around you may notice your trustworthy behavior if you maintain your commitments and avoid compromising someone's confidence, even if you actively despise them. Even if you learn the secret secondhand, don't assist spread it.

How To Look Approachable

It might be difficult to seem and feel at ease at parties, meetings, and other social gatherings. However, with time and work, you can establish a welcoming, open, and comfortable environment that will attract others and boost your social contacts. UOpenbody language, understanding how to engage people, and making an effort to seem more approachable help you look and feel more friendly.

Using Friendly Body Language

Smile often. A friendly, inviting grin may put everyone at ease and make you appear to be having a good time. People will notice your grin and assume you are polite, pleasant, and willing to engage in discussion. Studies have found Smiling lowers anxiety, blood pressure, and pulse rate, which will also put you at ease in social situations! Maintain an open stance. When people are uncomfortable in a circumstance, they physically isolate themselves from others. Take note of your posture. If you are scared or upset, tell yourself to stand straight, keep your arms at your sides, and lean toward those speaking to you. Reminding yourself to keep these postures can boost your mood and attract others to you.

When people speak, leaning toward them shows that you are engaged in what they are saying. Position your feet, legs, and body to face the speaker. This demonstrates to the speaker that you are actively listening to and engaged in their tale. When you're in a social scenario, don't fold your arms. When your arms are closed, you may convey negative signs such as "I'm too busy" or "Leave me alone." Other people will watch your body for signs, so pay attention to the cues you're exhibiting. Maintain constant eye contact. People will look around the room in social circumstances and likely discuss with someone if they make eye contact. Don't fix your gaze on the floor or your feet. To catch people's attention, look up and be aware of your surroundings.[103]

When someone approaches, smile and keep eye contact with them throughout the talk, and maintain eye contact for 7 to 10 seconds during a one-on-one talk. Maintain eye contact for 3 to 5 seconds during a group talk. This straightforward appearance will convey that you are trustworthy and interested in the subject. Don't twitch. It's fine to be frightened, bored, or upset, but avoid displaying negative feelings if you want to appear accessible. Fidgeting, such as shuffling back and forth, chewing your nails, twisting your hair, and other types of fidgeting, might indicate boredom, tension, or uneasiness. Recognize these patterns and take a few deep breaths whenever you need to fidget.

Avoid often touching your face with your hand. This might indicate that you are nervous. Tapping your feet might indicate frustration or boredom. People may believe you are uninterested in the discussion. Mirror the movements of the other individual. When conversing with someone at a party or event, observe their gestures, posture, and stance and try to imitate them. If that individual takes an open posture, you should as well. Try to imitate their energetic hand motions when narrating a narrative. Mirroring a person's body language may help create trust and establish a relationship when used selectively. When utilized correctly, it may assist build a pleasant connection and communicating to the other person that you like their presence. Before you replicate someone's body

---

[103] "The Power of Positive Thinking | Johns Hopkins Medicine." https://www.hopkinsmedicine.org/health/wellness-and-prevention/the-power-of-positive-thinking.

language, consider your connection with them. Avoid imitating someone in your position of authority. If you mimic your boss's body language during a meeting, people may perceive you as disrespectful and pushy.

Cultivating A Friendly Appearance

Create a welcoming wardrobe. Your clothing may help you appear nice and inviting, and appearing good can help you feel better about yourself. In a clothes store, ask a salesperson to assist you in selecting clothing options that are well-suited to you and appropriate for your body shape. Choosing flattering, well-tailored, and adaptable clothing will show others that you are composed, self-assured, and enjoyable to be around. Then, when you're feeling well, you'll appear happy! Wear clothing that flatters your physique and makes you feel good about yourself. For example, you may combine a tight top with loose-fitting jeans if you have broad shoulders.

At gatherings, dressing correctly communicates to others that you are courteous and delighted to be there. Make sure your attire is appropriate. Whether you are unclear about the formality of an event, ask the host respectfully if there is a dress code. Choose the appropriate hairdo. Ask a hairdresser what style would suit you best. They will advise you on what would look best with your hair texture and facial shape. Maintaining a well-groomed look can assist others in noticing you and signaling that you are calm and outgoing.

Wear hues that are accessible. Colors may have an impact on how others perceive and react to you. Wearing blues, greens, and warm earth tones like light yellow and beige can make you appear more approachable, dependable, and confident. People who wear red may appear more forceful, less accessible, and unfriendly than others. Colors that reflect a pleasant, inviting demeanor should be used in your attire. If you're heading to a social function, wear navy or green to put folks at ease. Accessorize your clothing with soothing, welcoming colors. Wear a green jacket when going to an informal brunch with a new set of friends to seem tranquil and pleasant. Make use of a name tag. Wear a name badge if you are at work or attending a business conference. People will see the name tag as an invitation to approach you and are more likely to strike up a discussion. This conveys your eagerness, openness, and readiness to engage in a conversation or network.

Conversing With Others

During a discussion, avoid distractions and interruptions. Listening helps develop the quality of your interactions with others and may assist indicate that you are pleasant and accessible. Allow the speaker to finish their thought or tale without interruption when engaging in a discussion. Maintain eye contact, smile, and nod to show that you are listening and paying attention to them. People will approach you for a chat if they see you be engaged and focused.

When you're chatting to someone, don't look at your phone. Be courteous and clear that you are listening and paying attention to the discourse. Focus on what the individual is saying. Don't get caught up in daydreams or distracted by other people's chats. Confirm the speaker's emotions. Be sympathetic and respond properly when someone shares a sad or disturbing circumstance. Avoid questioning their emotional response and, unless expressly requested, avoid providing advice. The speaker may sometimes prefer to communicate emotion for support rather than direction. Support and understanding will help the speaker feel at ease around you. Others will notice and are more willing to engage you in conversation.[104][105]

If someone expresses concern about their sick dog, support their concerns. "I'm very sorry. You must be going through a terrible moment. When a pet is ill, I realize how stressful it may be." Demonstrate to the person that you are supportive and kind and understand their emotional response. Pose inquiries. Ask them to explain or elaborate if you don't understand a person's argument or want to learn more about their point of view on a certain subject. Demonstrate that you are paying attention to what they are saying and are eager to learn more. This will improve the quality of the dialogue. The speaker and those around you will notice your focus, making it simpler for others to approach you. It's also a good idea to ask inquiries when you know you have something in common with someone. " Jane informed me that you had lately visited Berlin. Years ago, I visited Berlin! What was your favorite part of your vacation?" Creating a common ground allows the dialogue to continue and grow.

---

[104] "Mind Over Matter: The Effects of Positive Thinking - Wright Foundation." 20 Jul. 2017, https://wrightfoundation.org/effects-of-positive-thinking/.

[105] "Benefits of positive thinking: 10 ways to improve life with optimism." 12 Apr. 2022, https://www.betterup.com/blog/positive-thinking-benefits.

CHAPTER-8

How to Win Friends and Influence People

Maintaining Your Appearance

Dress formally. Consider costumes. People dress up in costumes to present an image that others will recognize immediately, whether it's a zombie, a fireman, or a bride. The truth is that every garment you wear is a costume, even your everyday clothes. They reveal a lot about you to others who view them. Use your attire to portray an image of yourself that demonstrates the qualities people seek in a friend: confidence, happiness, and stability. In general, this means wearing clean, crisp, well-fitting clothes that are matched such that colors and patterns complement one another. This demonstrates that you value yourself enough to care about your appearance, are responsible enough to keep it up, and are self-assured enough not to conceal it. Maintain good hygiene. The distinction between poor and appropriate hygiene becomes clear at handshake distance and closer. If you want to connect with others, you'll need to get up close and personal, so keeping your body as clean and well-maintained as you keep your clothing is essential. Shower every day, wash your hair no less than three and no more than five times each week; brush your teeth twice daily, floss once daily; wash your face, comb or brush your hair, and apply deodorant every morning. Consider the long term, such as keeping your nails cut and, for males, keeping your facial hair correctly trimmed or shaven.

Women can opt to shave their underarm and leg hair based on personal desire but be warned that not shaving such areas is still considered a sign of weak self-image or self-discipline by certain individuals. It's still best to maintain them shaved smooth to reach the biggest possible audience. Take proper care of your hair. A professional salon or barbershop is the best place to get your hair cut, no matter how long or short. Even if you don't usually wear it that way at home, make sure you can always make it seem nice and smart. Keep your stuff. More precisely, the two most critical items you should maintain are your house and your automobile (assuming you have one). You never know when you'll have unexpected visitors or who will view your bike or automobile as you enter or exit. Furthermore, keeping your surroundings clean might make you feel better about yourself.

Cars should be cleaned around monthly, cleaned of debris on the seats and floor, and regularly serviced for oil changes and tire rotation. Bicycles should be hand cleaned monthly (more if your bike becomes muddy or filthy) and tuned up at a bike shop twice a year. Your house should be kept as tidy as you possibly can. Clear the dishes and clean the kitchen after supper daily to avoid accumulation. Laundry should be washed as frequently as possible, and it should be folded and stored once it is clean. Rake your yard regularly to keep it clear of debris. Maintain a clean path and driveway.

Maintain control of your body language. Body language is strong communication between people, as has been said several times. This is since it is difficult to falsify and reveals much about our emotional states from moment to moment. Observing a person's body language as they talk might reveal more about that individual than the words they are uttering in many situations. That's why it's critical to do everything you can to utilize your body language to tell others what they want to know about you. Body language is complicated and context-sensitive: the same action or posture can have diverse meanings depending on who shows it, where it is displayed, and when it is displayed. Rather than attempting to interpret everyone else's body language, strive to make yours easy to read. [106]

Move confidently and without hesitating. When shaking someone's hand, squeeze it firmly - you'll be shocked how many people notice. Walk at your own pace, without hunching your shoulders or walking gently. Swing your arms as you walk. Take note of your posture. Every third-grade teacher has said it before, but appropriate posture is critical. Your shoulders should be slightly back from your chest to avoid hunching forward. Your neck should follow the line

---

[106] "Benefits of positive thinking: 10 ways to improve life with optimism." 12 Apr. 2022, https://www.betterup.com/blog/positive-thinking-benefits.

of your spine, and your chin should not protrude forward. Proper posture conveys confidence and self-esteem, helps you breathe more freely, and lowers your chances of chronic back discomfort as you age.

Make the most of your face. Always try your best to smile sincerely, establish ample eye contact (particularly while people are talking to you), and allow your face to be animated, communicating sincerity and empathy. People would prefer to be around someone who is always smiling and laughing than someone who is always serious or distant. Continue to be active. Even a sick body gains an air of health when its owner consistently strives to revitalize it. Exercise regularly and eat minimally. If you're having problems creating a timetable, remember that any effort is better than no effort. Even a few minutes of exercise after waking up or returning home from work will help you maintain your posture, manage your body language, and have more energy.

Winning Hearts And Minds

Brush up on your classical rhetorical principles. Aristotle is one of the few public speakers who has had a lasting impact on the Western world. His method of rhetoric, written over 2000 years ago, remains one of the most valuable frameworks for determining how to optimize the persuasiveness of whatever you want to communicate. Aristotle divides any compelling argument into three essential parts. Mixing all of them harmoniously may create a very difficult-to-resist appeal or argument. Using logos, you may build a firm foundation. The clarity, order and internal consistency of what you wish to express are represented through logos. Speech with logos cannot be twisted to imply anything other than what you want it to signify. Any attempt by a skeptic to do so will simply make them appear dumb.

By using ethos, you may increase credibility and believability. Ethos is the ethical underpinning of your argument, which generally is represented in your tone and style of delivery, as well as your presence of a character (and reputation if you're lucky enough to have a good one). As a result, ethos-based speech never throws doubt on your beliefs and maintains the belief that your words are trustworthy. Pathos will help you connect with your audience. Pathos is the component of your argument that connects it to the listener's personal life, experience, sentiments, and imagination. Speech with a lot of pathos properly makes your issue as much about them as it is about you by eliciting sympathetic feelings in your audience, prompting them to feel emotionally invested in anything you say. Finally, active listening should be practiced. Being a good listener makes people like you faster, but there's more to it than just sitting silently and watching the other person's lips move. Being an active listener entails employing specific techniques that demonstrate your focus on the speaker. These methods will become a natural part of your communication repertoire with practice.

When there is a suitable pause, even in the middle of a phrase, prompt the speaker with a little noise, such as "yes" or "mm-hmm." Don't go overboard, or you'll come across as impatient. Once every few phrases are plenty. You should always ask a question to get the speaker to go into more detail. Avoid interrupting the speaker while speaking, but do so as quickly as possible. This demonstrates that you are so taken with the speaker's remarks that you desire further information. Make use of neutral affirmation. Think about how the speaker feels about coming up with an answer when unsure what to make of a narrative or if you agree with it. If the speaker looks at you as if they can't believe what you're saying, agree with them by responding, "wow, that's insane," or something similar that helps you bond with the speaker without selecting a side. Ask the speaker what they thought of the narrative or how they felt about it when it is over. After a lengthier tale, people want to summarize their opinions. Re-summarize the tale once it has been summarized and hurl it back at the speaker. This demonstrates to the speaker that you listened and understood what they were saying, and they would appreciate it. You may then express your view to continue driving the debate. For example, assume someone informs you about their pet having to go to the vet due to an emergency. After the narrative is over, "So your cat had (medical problem)? But at the very least, you got him to the vet on time."

Personal anecdotes should be used sparingly. You're most likely attempting to be sympathetic and empathetic, but the listener will soon assume you'd rather speak about yourself than listen to anybody else. So use personal stories and anecdotes with caution. Speak clearly. Most people believe their voices are fixed in stone, but this is not the case. Even though you can't switch from soprano to baritone, you do have a surprising amount of influence on the overall tone of your voice and the clarity of your words when speaking. Sing to learn how to manage your voice. Simply singing aloud is one of the finest methods to train your voice. Try singing in the car or while performing chores at home. Through repetition, you'll gradually develop more control over the noises your throat creates.[107][108]

Speak with low-register tones that are smooth and round. This does not imply that you should strive to deepen your voice; rather, envision a greater space at the back of your lips and throat when speaking, and talk to fill it. Do not speak via your nose or a narrow, firmly compressed throat channel. Make sure you have lots of volumes. No need to roar when you talk; neither should you speak humbly. Do not mute your voice. It makes you more difficult to comprehend and might make you appear less confident in yourself. Make use of appealing wording. Just because people comprehend your words doesn't guarantee they understand what you're saying. There are excellent and awful ways to communicate what you have to say, as anybody who has clashed with a cousin or lover over a misinterpretation knows. You may learn to voice your opinion in a way that avoids upsetting or intimidating the listener, even

Using "I" language is all about assuming responsibility for oneself. As a substitute for blaming the other person for "making" you feel or act a certain way during an argument, say something like this instead: "When you (said/did/whatever), I felt..." It may appear foolish on paper, but it works effectively in a genuine fight since it prevents the other person from receiving more blame. Instead of stating, "When you said that, it made me angry," try "When you said that, I felt angry." This phrase may be used to express almost any

---

[107] "Ultimate Positive Thinking Toolkit: 19 Techniques & Exercises." 03 Jan. 2022, https://positivepsychology.com/positive-thinking-exercises/.

[108] "11 Benefits of Positive Thinking and What are They." https://positiveaffirmationscenter.com/benefits-of-positive-thinking/.

disagreement: "I felt like you were...," "I feel when you...," and so on.

The goal of "we" language is to make the other person feel included and relevant. Use "we" and "us" wording when discussing opportunities, events, or group work to solidify your peers' devotion and convey loyalty to those above you on the social or professional ladder. Instead of saying, "Do you want to hang out with me this weekend?" say, "We should get together this weekend!" This puts the other person on an equal footing with you and gives them control over the opportunity. Giving people power is a proven method to regain power since people will be much more willing to bend and flex for you when they repay the favor if they recall their previous contacts with you in a good and empowering light. Match beats with those around you. Every time they appear to "charm" someone into altering their mind or breaking the rules a little bit, stage and street hypnotists alike employ this strong tactic to spectacular effect. In theory, there isn't much to this method, but it takes practice to become proficient with it

Begin the discussion with brief "in" and easy inquiries to get the other person started. Pay close attention to accents, vocal tics (such as "like" and "uh"), and overall phrasing as you employ your active listening abilities. Respond to the other person's vocal tics and patterns while you continue to beg for what you want. Feel free to borrow some of their accents, but don't make a parody. Speaking in the manner of others puts them at ease and quietly says that they can trust you since you are similar to them in some indefinable way.

Match everything you see about the other person's body language. Is he shifting his weight from one foot to the other? Is she tapping one finger or all of them while waiting for the computer to load?

You may combine these little details to form an even stronger empathetic link. Show off your nice character. You should strive for important characteristics: helpfulness, friendliness, excitement, bravery, and dependability. These are the characteristics that everyone searches for in others, the characteristics that make you someone people want to trust and listen to. They begin with personal honesty and determination and are difficult to imitate. However, if you concentrate on them, you may teach yourself to display them more frequently and freely than previously.[109]

Every day, affirm yourself. It may sound ridiculous, but self-affirmation is effective. Simply think about the good characteristics you wish to embody and repeat them to yourself a few times. Tell yourself you have them: "I am a compassionate person," "I am an enthusiastic person," and so on. Next, look for opportunities to show off your best talents. We often pass up the bolder option in favor of the one that would draw less attention because we are uncomfortable with the scenario. Combat this by reminding yourself to keep your eyes open for instances when you are going to be dismissive or disrespectful. When you notice you're going to become that sad, tired person, force yourself to be the person everyone wants to be around. If it doesn't make any difference, it's great mental training. You'll eventually absorb it.

---

[109] "Positive Thinking - How It Impacts Your Life | happiness.com." https://www.happiness.com/positive-thinking/.

CHAPTER-9

Love Your Enemies

"**Y**ou should love your adversaries and pray for those who are trying to harm you." is one of the Bible's most important moral directives (Matthew 5:44). (Matthew 5:44). The larger context for this appeal is to draw closer to God, who "raises His sun on the righteous and the bad." But how can you use this directive in your daily life? Compassion and forgiveness for your adversaries may be extremely beneficial not just to them but also to yourself.

Forgiving Your Enemies

Consider what made you enemies. This may be a terrible set of memories to revisit, but it is vital to do so to shift your mindset. What part did you play in your title? How long have you had a falling out? Remembering these factors will assist you in finally reaching an agreement with your adversaries. Maintain modest expectations. The expression "love your enemies" doesn't imply you have to love them like you love your friends or family. You should be able to treat them as equals, as the Bible says that God bestows his benefits on everybody equally. Third, understand if you require further time. If your adversary has badly injured you, such as a buddy who had an affair with your spouse or a coworker who wrecked a professional chance for you, it may be difficult to forgive them.[110][111]

Accept that you will not receive an apology. You may assume that for your adversaries to forgive you fully, they must repent for their wrongdoings against you. However, this provides your adversary with significant leverage. Recognize that forgiving and loving your adversary benefits you more than they do. Discover the health advantages of forgiving. It's possible to lower your blood pressure, alleviate symptoms of anxiety or despair, and even enhance your immune system when you forgive someone. Getting rid of bitterness may also improve your mental health by increasing your self-esteem and enhancing your psychological well-being.

Make forgiving a conscious decision. When you have bitter or resentful thoughts about your adversary, stop and think about something good instead. Consider how you have evolved in your interactions with your adversary rather than how furious you remain with them. Remember that you maintain your victim status when you have hostile feelings against your adversaries. If you can't adore

---

[110] ""Love Your Enemies" What Jesus Really Meant - Christianity." 04 Oct. 2019, https://www.christianity.com/wiki/christian-life/what-does-it-mean-to-love-your-enemies.html.

[111] "How To Love Your Enemies (6 Practical Tips) - Rethink." 22 Feb. 2021, https://www.rethinknow.org/how-to-love-your-enemies/.

them immediately, attempt to ignore them or think about them from a neutral perspective.

Showing Compassion To Your Enemy

Demonstrate empathy for your adversary. What types of previous experiences could have influenced their behavior? Are they going through anything you're not aware of? Recognize your shortcomings. Consider moments when you said something nasty or improper. In a similar position, would you desire forgiveness? When have you previously been forgiven? How did the individual show their empathy or care for you? Keep a journal of your thoughts. If you are resentful, keep a notebook or a meditation book to record your thoughts. You should consider praying aloud to hear your thoughts if you are religious.

Rethink your connection with your adversary. If your adversary is someone you must engage with every day (such as a coworker), try to see every interaction as a chance to bridge the schism between you. Be gentle and patient with them, and show an interest in their progress. Suppose you don't want to reconcile with your adversary, at least attempt to view your interactions as a method to retain basic respect for them. Be cordial in your encounters with them; welcome them when you meet them and congratulate them on important achievements.

Finding New Allies

Help a good cause by volunteering. If you have experienced a serious tragedy, such as the murder of a family member, working for a larger cause, such as victim advocacy groups, may help you find peace. This encounter will also introduce you to others who have been harmed in similar ways. In addition, it will provide you with a community where you may turn for help. Build strong relationships with your peers. Focusing on more good connections might be an effective method to show love towards your opponent. Invite a new acquaintance for a cup of coffee or a beer after work to get to know each other better. You may also join groups and meet others with similar hobbies, such as hiking clubs, photography clubs, or writing workshops. Look for clubs that meet in community centers, libraries, or universities in your area. Finally, make use of counseling services. If you have trouble putting your faith in new people, consider seeing a therapist who can teach you how to build trust and recover from betrayal. A therapist can also help you through the process of forgiving and moving on from the grief of your relationships with your adversary.

How To Deal With Enemies

Enemies and haters may be bothersome, and their words and insults might disturb you. Learning to deal with it entails confronting your own projected anxieties as well as seeing the human being in the other person.

Finding Out Why The Hate Is Happening

Ask them calmly and gently if you don't understand why they dislike you, But don't approach your hater if you know they're capable of doing something dramatic or hurtful to you. It might also cause you shame. If they are rude, start swearing at you, or get aggressive, go away and don't try to talk to them again until they become citizens. Some individuals can be given second opportunities to see that you aren't a nasty person and that they have no reason to detest you. However, some individuals will never like you, so don't waste your time worrying about why they don't.[112][113]

Responding To The Enemy

If you understand why people dislike you, act maturely and apologize if it was your fault. Although it is understandable to feel hate and refuse to accept responsibility for one's actions, the only person who can solve an issue is the one who caused it in the first place. If they refuse to accept your apology, there isn't much else you can do but ignore them. Respect them like you would your friends; if they require assistance, assist them. This will demonstrate to them that you are pleasant and kind. Give them compliments while avoiding being unpleasant, and don't condemn them if they respond negatively. If these things don't work out, inform your friends so they can console you, take a big breath, and try again. Never get offended, but if you are, keep your cool. When things become fouled up, restrain yourself or find excuses to get out of the situation rather than losing your mind attempting to resolve things. Treat your "adversary" with respect and observe whether they reply rationally. If not, people will see that you tried, and some (maybe the majority) will appreciate you. The other folks are the ones who deserve to be respected.

Stop aiding if you try to help those who are ostensibly unfriendly, and they respond unkindly. This simply encourages them to take

---

[112] ""Love Your Enemies!" What Does It Mean? Can It Be Done?." https://gratefulness.org/resource/love-your-enemies/.

[113] "Love Your Enemies: What It Means And Examples On How To Do So - Pray." 27 Apr. 2021, https://www.pray.com/articles/love-your-enemies-what-it-means-and-examples-on-how-to-do-so.

advantage of your generosity. Instead, give your adversaries not a single ounce of your energy. If you help anyone, including your opponents, you may provide something to someone who doesn't "deserve" it.

Ignore everything this individual says. They're probably simply criticizing you out of jealousy. Whatever people say can't offend you unless you allow it. Remember that they want you to respond when they say anything hurtful to you. Assume you didn't hear it. Don't thank them or pay them any attention to it. If they continue to insult you or annoy you in any way, go away. Do not look at them or speak to them; simply walk away. They'll probably become bored and quit picking on you after a few times of this. When you've exhausted all possible solutions, hand things over to the cosmos and walk away (mentally, if you can't physically go). They have their problems to deal with. Ignore them and concentrate on your strengths and excellent qualities. Remember that you can't please everyone all of the time. It's not feasible. If this individual becomes aggressive towards you or continues to insult or disturb you, and ignoring them isn't working, inform them that their conduct is bothering you and that they have no cause for it. If they continue, you will have to learn to quit getting angered by their statements and accept that anything they say is most likely a lie. Surround yourself with people that accept you for who you are. These individuals will boost your self-esteem, and you should recognize that it doesn't matter what detractors say as long as you have excellent friends on your side.

How To Avoid Making Enemies

Work, education, and personal relationships may all fail. Disagreements can escalate into long-term animosity, while other individuals may just decide that they loathe something about you. Everyone will inevitably encounter one of these exhausting relationships at some time. As long as they aren't fully developed, you don't have to wait for them to mature. The best way to prevent enemies is to deal with difficult situations head-on and create healthy connections.

Building Positive Relationships

Demonstrate interest in others. People frequently go through life without considering how their demeanor will appear to or affect others. Try to demonstrate to others that you regard them as equals and care about them. When meeting new individuals, ask my questions and make eye contact to demonstrate that you're interested. Express your admiration for someone's accomplishments and talents. Encourage others to share their thoughts and views. This shows that you regard their intelligence and insight. Bring up topics of interest and find out what they think about them. While you will be in charge of the conversation, you will also show that you appreciate what they have to say. Show compassion. Kindness is the most effective way to disarm people who may dislike you and set a civil tone for disagreements. According to studies, compassion is one of the most effective persuasive tactics.

Always be courteous, particularly when disagreeing. Keep an eye out for regular, inadvertently impolite conduct. Don't, for example, speak over others or patronize or talk down to them. Give a lot of praises while breaking the ice or encountering a pause in a conversation. Express your feelings on someone's attire, or whether you think them intriguing or knowledgeable. Take note of your body language throughout interactions. Maintaining eye contact and smiling will convey warmth and happiness to others around you. Control your bounds. Understanding what makes you upset and disagreeable is just as crucial for your emotional intelligence as understanding what makes others upset and disagreeable. Many bad personal relationships result from unmet expectations and an inability to explain them honestly.

Communicate your feelings openly and politely if you feel that someone is excessively familiar or that their conduct makes you uncomfortable. Avoid the urge to ignore them or give nonverbal cues since they are easily misread or ignored. If you believe someone is condescending to you, gently express your appreciation for their explanation while also indicating that you have your understanding of the issue.[114]

Defusing Confrontations

Take a rest. You must disperse any emotions that may serve as a distraction before you can constructively deal with a disagreement or argument. During confrontations, people frequently experience wrath and anxiety, which impairs their capacity to reason and weigh the ramifications of what they say. If you sense that someone is particularly upset with you, offer that you spend a few moments apart and schedule a time to meet to resolve your concerns. "I think we should take some time to cool off before we debate this further," say you. Take a break from the argument and consider something unrelated that makes you happy. Consider going to a beach or engaging in a pastime. When you return to your problem, you'll have a more positive outlook.

---

[114] "Luke 6:27-36 NIV - Love for Enemies - "But to you who - Bible Gateway." https://www.biblegateway.com/passage/?search=Luke%206:27-36&version=NIV.

Maintain your composure. You will never be able to control how others see you fully, but you can control your reactions. An argument is less likely to escalate and harm you if you keep your cool. You may also discover that you make better and less emotional judgments when composting. There are several strategies to calm yourself down, such as counting to 10 or taking a deep breath. Don't be afraid to take as long as you need. Recognize their point of view. It might be tough to relate to someone with whom you actively disagree. Pose as them to have a better understanding of their feelings.

Even if you disagree with them, empathizing with their stance shows humility and respect on your behalf. This reduces the possibility of a single confrontation developing into long-term animosity. It could even be beneficial to ask them to clarify their point of view. "I'm trying to understand your side of this," say you. Mint maintain, that your cool and engaging in active listening is critical, so they know you value their viewpoint. You may also wish or need that your stance to be acknowledged. Comprehending their point of view does not absolve them from understanding yours. Inform them if you believe they don't grasp your point of view and offer to clarify your position. Avoid becoming defensive. In a disagreement, it is easy to get caught up in the argument and feel the need to fight for your position vehemently.

Keep your counter-arguments to a later time. This way, the other person can express themselves without being interrupted or threatened. Try to consider criticism and seek the truth in comments honestly. Even if your first instinct is to disregard this critique, giving it some thought will prevent you from reacting defensively. Seek independent opinions and mediation. Asking a friend or a neutral person to hear both sides and weigh in on a problem is a terrific method to get perspective. With a third party present, you and the individual you are arguing with are more likely to stay respectful and helpful. If the connection in issue is serious or essential to you, you may want to explore seeking the services of a therapist to seek a mutual settlement.

Dealing With People That Dislike You

Maintain a positive attitude. You can't always control whether or not people like you, so you just have to handle the issue and keep it from getting worse. If you can't escape an uncomfortable connection, focus on what is important: the job, a school assignment, or similar hobbies. Use these topics to keep the squabbling horrors at bay. Try starting a conversation about something unrelated to your dispute. When you return to the disputed issue, you may discover that other themes will rebuild the more favorable parts of your connection and create a more positive focus. It may be beneficial to clear the air, so the other person realizes you're focussing on more productive topics. "I know you're upset with me, but I think we should focus on what's most important," say you. Begin an open discussion about your differences. If you don't understand why someone dislikes you, respectfully and directly ask them. You could discover that the issues were merely a result of miscommunication and that all you needed to do was clear the air.[115]

Say something like, "I'd like to understand your issues better while also ensuring that you understand mine." Understand how to forgive. Even if you have been wronged, holding on to your anger

---

[115] "30 Bible verses about Loving Your Enemies - Knowing Jesus." https://bible.knowing-jesus.com/topics/Loving-Your-Enemies.

will not assist you. Hurt sentiments frequently lead to issues in future conflicts, so address your emotions first. Forgiveness will help you move on by reducing your concern about the issue. Forgiving does not always imply forgetting. If the harmful conduct continues, your relationship may be poisonous and should be ended. It may be difficult to forgive when there has been no recognition or apology. But that doesn't mean you should harbor grudges. Begin the reconciliation process. Tense relationships sometimes persist because neither person is prepared to take the initiative and make things better.

"What can we do to solve our problems?" First, invite them to air their complaints with you. Stay away from them. Not all relationships can be repaired or even improved. Hostility and confrontation are bad for everyone; if they become unavoidable, the best thing to do is make room for them. Say something like this: "I don't believe our relationship is healthy for either of us. We should either take some time apart or avoid each other." Depending on the circumstances, you may wish to notify a few close friends that you will be spending time apart from that individual to avoid a possibly problematic scenario.

CHAPTER-10

The Consequences Of Being Selfish

The Negative Effects Of Selfishness

Selfishness may negatively influence your personal life, work performance, and development. Selfishness in other areas, such as a leader, may wreak havoc on a team's productivity and engagement. People are often selfish because they believe they can profit from every situation. This is sometimes true regarding financial problems and the route to success. The polar opposite of selfishness has a negative influence on our lives as well. Selfishness and otherness can negatively impact our psychological well-being, interpersonal relationships, and physical health. Surprisingly, in some circumstances, otherness has advantages while selfishness has disadvantages. Being excessively selfish can lead to loneliness, manage you harsh and hostile to everyone you meet. Here are some of the most serious consequences of selfishness that might wreck your life.

Being selfish will lead to a lonely existence. These individuals dislike their lives and tend to drive others away in numerous ways, including hurting, insulting, or even embarrassing them regularly. This is one of the least appealing characteristics that will harm your reputation and lead to loneliness. Yet, selfish individuals continue to demand things from others. What matters to these folks is when something benefits them. Even feelings like love and caring or aiding friends have a cost; tiny to receive it back, or It makes no difference to them, even a deep relationship or friendship.[116][117]

They were being selfish means being more self-centered. They are unconcerned about others and place a high value on anything they endure or go through. This might lead to a more concerning personality and further psychological disorders. Selfish people are more likely to become addicted to drugs. People that are hooked on something are often self-centered. They believe they require everything and are the only ones who can manage their emotions; they believe they can begin or stop using these medications whenever they choose. Being selfish can be harmful to our loved ones. On the run to meet your demands, you may wind up harming the only individuals who have ever loved and stood behind you. This has ruined many families life.

All of the negative consequences of selfishness can only harm your life. Nevertheless, it is beneficial to be selfish at times in our lives.

---

[116] "A Speech on "The Negative Effects of Selfishness"."
https://writolay.com/negative-effects-of-selfishness/.
[117] "4 Ways Selfishness Ruins Your Life - RELEVANT."
https://relevantmagazine.com/life5/4-ways-selfishness-ruins-your-life/.

For example, there are a few moments when we must think for ourselves and then make the proper option; this is not being selfish, but rather being selfless. One of the most effective strategies to mitigate selfishness is to cultivate compassion in our hearts. Being nice to others may help you maintain a positive mental, social, and familial life. Kindness is the most endearing human character quality that may be transmitted and shared with thousands of people without the expectation of compensation.

Selfishness Is Not Sustainable

In today's social and political context, we may frequently wonder, "How can people be so selfish?" We are not only in the middle of a worldwide epidemic that demands a full-community effort to contain and battle, but we are also dealing with systematic injustices and social divides that continue to pull people apart. To strive for betterment, we must not only address the underlying causes of selfishness but also take action to modify our conduct and inspire others to do the same.

Almost everything we do or say impacts others, either directly or indirectly. As a result, activities that are selfish, charitable, or somewhere in between are all examples of social conduct. When we think of selfishness, we truly mean antisocial acts or those harmful to social relationships and violate social standards. Conversely, prosocial (altruistic) acts promote social relationships and conform to social standards. On the other hand, selfish actions are more generous and unselfish, wet and prevent harm or benefit others.

Before delving into the repercussions of selfish action, it is critical to understand that selfishness is not necessarily intrinsically evil. Scientists differentiate between healthy and unhealthy selfishness. The former is necessary for self-preservation and includes setting boundaries and knowing when to prioritize yourself. In contrast, the latter can be harmful and includes exploitation and disregard for others (Kaufman & Jauk, 2020). There will always be times when you should prioritize yourself to benefit your emotional and physical well-being. Still, you may expect unfavorable results when your actions routinely harm others. Reduced prosociality has been linked to an increase in "deviant" (socially unacceptable/undesirable) conduct, which can impair social connections (Pletzer et al., 2018). Concerning yourself primarily with relationships and other encounters may make your counterpart feel disregarded, straining your relationship. Because social support influences physical, mental, and professional health, constant stress in relationships will harm both parties in the long term (Uchino et al., 2012). From a leadership standpoint, perceived selfishness and pride frequently negatively impact staff collaboration (Ritzenhöfer et al., 2019). but generally, displaying gratitude and concern for one's followers or workers is regarded as valued; as a result, selfish actions can inhibit succcssful lcadcrship.

How To Stop Being Selfish

Everyone is susceptible to selfishness from time to time. Selfishness is encouraged by many facets of our culture, but it can cause harm to others for little or no benefit to the self. A selfish person also loses friends or loved ones because, no matter how charming or intriguing a selfish person is, maintaining a connection with a selfish person is difficult. A selfish individual would never believe themselves to be selfish. Many people believe that selfishness and pride are admirable traits and that putting the needs of others ahead of your own is for losers. There are various things you may do if you're concerned about being too selfish and wish to move toward thankfulness and humility—experiment with putting yourself last. If you're selfish, you're probably constantly aiming for #1 first. You need to make a change as soon as possible if you want to start living a life filled with happiness and free of selfishness. Stop the next time you're doing anything, whether standing in line at a buffet or waiting for a bus seat, and let others have what they want first, whether it's food, comfort, or ease. Don't be that person always thinking "me, me, me" who demands to have everything first. Remember that other individuals are just as unique as you are and that they, too, deserve to receive what they desire.[118]

This week, make it a goal to be the last person to leave the room in three different circumstances. Of course, after you've leveled out, you shouldn't constantly put yourself last since you can end yourself in a scenario where others take advantage of you. However, it is an excellent habit if you always put yourself first. If you can't place yourself last even once, you may have an issue you're aware of.[119]

Put yourself in the shoes of someone else. Walking a mile in another person's shoes can alter your life for the rest of your life. Of course, you won't be able to accomplish this, but you may think about the people around you and how they could fit in any given

---

[118] "The Danger of Selfishness."
https://www.selfgrowth.com/articles/The_Danger_of_Selfishness.html.
[119] "Selfishness Effects and causes in Human Nature - Actforlibraries.org."
http://www.actforlibraries.org/selfishness-effects-and-causes-in-human-nature/.

circumstance. Consider how your mother, friend, employer, or a random person on the street may be feeling before you act, and you may discover that the world isn't as cut and dried as you imagined. The more you cultivate empathy and ponder what other people are going through, the easier it will be to let go of your selfishness. For example, consider how your waitress could be feeling before you start shouting at her for taking the erroneous order. She may be fatigued from standing for ten hours in a row, overwhelmed by having to work too many tables, or just depressed about something else; is it essential for you to make her feel horrible only to obtain what you want?

Keep in mind that you aren't more significant than everyone else. Self-centered people believe they are the center of the universe and the world should revolve around them. That notion, like a bad habit, must be abandoned. Whether you're Madonna or Donna the hairdresser, you should see yourself as equal to everyone else, not as superior because you have more money, better beauty, or more ability than the person next to you. Make an effort to be humble and modest. You are only a small part of the vast and amazing world. Don't assume you deserve more than others just because you're "you."

Don't let your past shape your present. Okay, so your friends, coworkers, and neighbors may regard you as the most selfish person in the world. It may be tough for you to break free from that pattern or for others to see you as anything other than what they anticipated you to be. Stop thinking that way and instead learn to move on and become a new person. Others who know you may be astonished that you're being selfless or that you've quit stressing over yourself; this motivates you, even more, to keep being selfless. When you strive to do something usable, others may doubt your reasons. This should motivate you to be less selfish even more frequently. Don't give up; believe you were born selfish and can't change.[120][121][122]

---

[120] "Good, Neutral, and Bad Selfishness | Psychology Today." 15 Jan. 2015, https://www.psychologytoday.com/us/blog/cui-bono/201501/good-neutral-and-bad-selfishness.

[121] "Your Selfishness as a Spouse Has a Three-Fold Negative Effect." 15 Jul. 2019, https://www.loveandrespect.com/blog/your-selfishness-as-a-spouse-has-a-three-fold-negative-effect/.

[122] "What are the disadvantages of selfishness? - Quora." https://www.quora.com/What-are-the-disadvantages-of-selfishness.

Conclusion

Sacrifices are typically required when two valuable things cannot coexist, and one must be given up for the sake of the other. But not all sacrifices are self-sacrifices. For example, someone who gives up something that benefits them for a larger benefit to themselves—say, abandoning the luxury of a large house to live in a modest apartment closer to work—makes a sacrifice but not self-sacrifice. This definition has some deliberate ambiguity because 'constitute,' 'benefit,' and matter to' are all possible options. Something is said to constitute someone if it is their own or a component of what they are. If someone gives their life, or, for example, their memories, limbs or organs, dignity, identity, integrity, or basic capacities, they are sacrificing something that comprises the self.

In the context of one's self-interest, a given thing is beneficial. When someone gives up an opportunity to get a job interview, money, or physical comfort, they are seen as sacrificing. When something is important to someone, it means they care about it, respect it, love it, or are dedicated to it. If people can be required to make specific self-sacrifice, they may be obligated to sacrifice something significant to them; in fact, they may be obligated to sacrifice something more important to them than everything else.

For example, parents who support their adult kid's decision to join in a risky, even life-threatening humanitarian intervention are prepared to sacrifice their child, whom they love more than anything else, for the sake of the intervention's noble ideals. The individual who decides to participate in this type of dangerous activity takes self-sacrifice (of their safety and maybe their lives), but so do those who love them, by sacrificing what means most to them for the benefit of someone or something else. What characterizes the self or what helps the self may or may not be important to the self. And what matters to the self may or may not constitute or benefit the self. Even though what characterizes or benefits the self is important to the self, someone or something else may be more important.

If we were psychological egoists, only ourselves(or our well-being, or whatever) would be non-instrumentally important to us; everything we valued would either (partly) constitute or benefit ourselves. However, we (or, at least, most of us) are not psychological egoists; we normally value egoistic, altruistic, and unbiased ways. That is why something that does not define or benefit us in a purely self-interested sense may be important. When we regard something (or someone) more than yourselves, and we are forced to choose between what constitutes or benefits ourselves and what means most to us, we may choose to safeguard what matters most to us rather than yourselves. This would seem clear to any parent who has worked to exhaustion for their child to have a better life or who knows and would gladly die for their child. As long as we can see that what we care about is of the utmost importance to us, even if it is dreadful, we may justifiably sacrifice for what we care about, even if it is a terrible sacrifice.

Cases of self-sacrifice are tricky because people may not regard themselves or anything else that is important to them in the way they should. They may overvalue or underestimate their worth; whatever (or anyone) else means the most to them may not be what (or who) truly matters the most. This may result in self-sacrificing when they should not or failing to self-sacrifice when they should.

We should not assume that what is important to us is also important to others. When anything goes wrong while generating our values, we should be skeptical of the values that result. For example, women trained to be particularly self-sacrificing by oppressive gender standards may not appreciate themselves enough because something went wrong in how their values were formed. "Do-gooders" may have a similarly self-sacrificing set of values, not because of forced gender norms but because of pathological altruism. Others, on the other hand, err in the opposite direction, acting in ways that unfairly benefit their own families while failing to engage politically to make the mechanisms of opportunity hoarding unavailable. In this latter scenario, maybe worrying about how individuals they care about will fare under more equitable rules taints how values are created.

References

"21 Selfish People Traits And What To Learn From Them (2022)." https://www.coaching-online.org/selfish-people/

"10 Great Ways to Deal with Selfish People - Lifehack." https://www.lifehack.org/articles/communication/10-great-ways-deal-with-selfish-people.html.

"4 Ways to Deal With Selfish People | Psychology Today." https://www.psychologytoday.com/us/blog/the-couch/201403/4-ways-deal-selfish-people.

"11 Habits Toxic Coworkers Have In Common To Watch Out For In ... - Bustle." https://www.bustle.com/articles/188879-11-habits-toxic-coworkers-have-in-common-to-watch-out-for-in-the-office.

"Altruism Definition & Meaning - Merriam-Webster." https://www.merriam-webster.com/dictionary/altruism.

"What Is Altruism? - Verywell Mind." https://www.verywellmind.com/what-is-altruism-2794828.

"Altruism - Wikipedia." https://en.wikipedia.org/wiki/Altruism.

"Altruism | Psychology Today." 19 Oct. 2012, https://www.psychologytoday.com/us/basics/altruism.

"Altruism Definition | What Is Altruism - Greater Good." https://greatergood.berkeley.edu/topic/altruism/definition.

"Altruism Definition & Meaning - Merriam-Webster." https://www.merriam-webster.com/dictionary/altruism.

"What Is Altruism? - Verywell Mind."
     https://www.verywellmind.com/what-is-altruism-2794828.

"Altruism - Wikipedia." https://en.wikipedia.org/wiki/Altruism.

"Altruism | Psychology Today." 19 Oct. 2012,
     https://www.psychologytoday.com/us/basics/altruism.

"Altruism Definition | What Is Altruism - Greater Good."
     https://greatergood.berkeley.edu/topic/altruism/definition.

"Altruism (Stanford Encyclopedia of Philosophy)." 25 Aug. 2016,
     https://plato.stanford.edu/entries/altruism/.

"What Is Altruism? Examples and Types of Altruistic Behavior." 24
     May. 2022, https://psychcentral.com/health/altruism-examples.

"What Is Altruism in Psychology? 8 Inspiring Examples." 03 Sept.
     2020, https://positivepsychology.com/altruism/.

"Altruism: Meaning, Examples, Types, Benefits, and More."
     https://mantracare.org/therapy/what-is/altruism/.

"Altruism - Ethics Unwrapped."
     https://ethicsunwrapped.utexas.edu/glossary/altruism.

"What Is Altruism (and Is It Important at Work)? - BetterUp." 19
     Oct. 2021, https://www.betterup.com/blog/altruism.

"What Is Altruism, and Why Is It Important? | Teachers College,
     Columbia ...." 15 Dec. 2011,
     https://www.tc.columbia.edu/articles/2011/december/what-is-
     altruism-and-why-is-it-important/.

"The truth about altruism - Harvard Health." 05 Jan. 2016,
     https://www.health.harvard.edu/blog/the-truth-about-altruism-
     201601058929.

"ALTRUISM | meaning in the Cambridge English Dictionary." https://dictionary.cambridge.org/dictionary/english/altruism.

"Altruism: Characteristics, Theories and Advantages." https://itspsychology.com/altruism/.

"115 Synonyms & Antonyms of ALTRUISM - Merriam-Webster." https://www.merriam-webster.com/thesaurus/altruism.

"30 Top Pros & Cons Of Altruism - E&C." https://environmental-conscience.com/altruism-pros-cons/.

"Altruism definition, types and examples - Toolshero." 10 Feb. 2022, https://www.toolshero.com/sociology/altruism/.

"Altruism - The Decision Lab." https://thedecisionlab.com/reference-guide/philosophy/altruism.

"Altruism Magazine | Altru Health System." https://www.altru.org/about-us/altruism-magazine/.

"Generosity Definition & Meaning - Merriam-Webster." https://www.merriam-webster.com/dictionary/generosity.

"What Is Generosity? (And How to Be a More Generous Person)." 04 Feb. 2019, https://www.psychologytoday.com/us/blog/click-here-happiness/201902/what-is-generosity-and-how-be-more-generous-person.

"What is Generosity? - the University of Notre Dame." https://generosityresearch.nd.edu/more-about-the-initiative/what-is-generosity/.

"What Is Generosity? - The Spiritual Life." https://slife.org/what-is-generosity/.

"What Is Generosity? - ChurchPlanting.com." 16 Jul. 2012, https://www.churchplanting.com/what-is-generosity/.

"55 Synonyms & Antonyms of GENEROSITY - Merriam-Webster." https://www.merriam-webster.com/thesaurus/generosity.

"Generosity: Anyone Can Learn to Be Generous - WebMD." https://www.webmd.com/balance/features/how-to-be-more-generous.

"What is generosity? - Quora." 29 Apr. 2017, https://www.quora.com/What-is-generosity.

"What Is Generosity? (And How to Be a More Generous Person)." https://www.psychologytoday.com/au/blog/click-here-happiness/201902/what-is-generosity-and-how-be-more-generous-person.

"Generosity vs Giving. What Does It Mean to Be Generous?." https://www.mindfulschools.org/personal-practice/what-does-it-mean-to-be-generous/.

"Generosity | SkillsYouNeed." https://www.skillsyouneed.com/ps/generosity.html.

"Generosity - Definition, Meaning & Synonyms | Vocabulary.com." https://www.vocabulary.com/dictionary/generosity.

"What Is Generosity? - The Spiritual Life." https://slife.org/generosity/.

"Generosity Definition & Meaning | Dictionary.com." https://www.dictionary.com/browse/generosity.

"What is Generosity? - Faith+Lead." 28 Jul. 2015, https://faithlead.luthersem.edu/what-is-generosity/.

"Generosity – Concept, importance, examples and phrases." https://conceptdaily.com/generosity-concept-importance-examples-and-phrases/.

"Generosity - Wikipedia." https://en.wikipedia.org/wiki/Generosity.

"How to Love Your Kids (with Pictures) - wikiHow." 06 May. 2021, https://www.wikihow.com/Love-Your-Kids.

"35 Simple Ways To Love Your Child In Everyday Life." https://amotherfarfromhome.com/love-your-child/.

"12 Ways to Love Your Wayward Child | Desiring God." 09 May. 2007, https://www.desiringgod.org/articles/12-ways-to-love-your-wayward-child.

[1] "5 Secrets to Love Your Child Unconditionally | Psychology Today." 02 Mar. 2014, https://www.psychologytoday.com/us/blog/peaceful-parents-happy-kids/201403/5-secrets-love-your-child-unconditionally.

"How to Love Your Kids Unconditionally - Crosswalk.com." 02 Apr. 2013, https://www.crosswalk.com/family/parenting/teens/how-to-love-your-kids-unconditionally.html.

"Teaching Children How To Love - freemansperspective.com." 31 Jan. 2022, https://freemansperspective.com/teaching-children-how-to-love/.

"6 Practical Ways to Show Unconditional Love to Kids." 12 Feb. 2020, https://www.thearkgroup.org/blog/unconditional-love.

"How to Explain Love to Little Kids - Fatherly." 13 Feb. 2018, https://www.fatherly.com/love-money/how-to-explain-love-to-little-kids.

"3 Ways to Be Loved by Little Kids - wikiHow." 05 Aug. 2020, https://www.wikihow.com/Be-Loved-by-Little-Kids.

"15 Ways You Can Show Your Kids You Love Them — Every Day." 25 Jun. 2018, https://www.huffpost.com/entry/15-ways-you-can-show-your-kids-you-love-themevery_b_5b1ac57be4b0253c28270715.

"5 Ways to Show Love to Your Children - for the family." https://forthefamily.org/5-ways-show-love-children/.

"Four Parenting Tips on How to Love Your Children Equally." 26 May. 2020, https://goodlifedetroit.com/parenting-tips-love-your-children-equally/.

"13 Ways To Raise Kids Who Love And Care For Each Other." https://www.lifehack.org/articles/lifestyle/13-ways-raise-kids-who-love-and-care-for-each-other.html.

"16 Parenting Rules That Teach Us How to Really Love a Child." 11 Mar. 2022, https://www.creativehealthyfamily.com/how-to-really-love-a-child-parenting/.

"How to Love Your Child When You Can't Even Love Yourself - Purpose Fairy." https://www.purposefairy.com/97372/love-your-child-love-yourself/.

"72 Incredibly Simple Ways to Show Love for Children." 10 Feb. 2021, https://parentswithconfidence.com/72-incredibly-simple-ways-to-show-love-for-children/.

"HOW TO LOVE A CHILD - Janusz Korczak."
http://www.januszkorczak.ca/legacy/3_How%20to%20Love%20a%20Child.pdf.

"11 Simple Ways to Show Your Child Your Love - Parents." 02 Mar. 2022, https://www.parents.com/parenting/better-parenting/simple-ways-to-show-your-child-your-love/.

"100 Ways to Show Your Children You Love Them Deeply." 26 Aug. 2021, https://joannabel.com/100-ways-to-show-your-children-you-love-them/.

"How to Love like a Child | HuffPost Communities." 30 Jan. 2013, https://www.huffpost.com/entry/how-to-love_b_2537774.

"How to achieve a positive attitude - Harvard Health." 12 Apr. 2017, https://www.health.harvard.edu/mind-and-mood/how-to-achieve-a-positive-attitude.

"What Is the Meaning of Positive Attitude – Definitions." https://www.successconsciousness.com/blog/positive-attitude/what-is-the-meaning-of-positive-attitude/.

"Positive Attitude: Definition, Examples, & Strategies." https://www.berkeleywellbeing.com/develop-positive-attitude.html.

"10 Creative Ways to Keep a Positive Attitude No Matter What." 29 Apr. 2021, https://blog.hubspot.com/service/positive-attitude.

"10 Tips for Maintaining a Positive Attitude | Indeed.com." 12 Dec. 2019, https://www.indeed.com/career-advice/career-development/how-to-keep-a-positive-attitude.

"Why You Need a Positive Attitude and How to Gain It."
    https://www.successconsciousness.com/blog/positive-
    attitude/positive-attitude/.

"What Is A Positive Attitude and Why Is It Important?." 19 Feb.
    2020, https://veteransaffiliatesuccess.com/what-is-a-positive-
    attitude-and-why-is-it-important/.

"15 Tips for Maintaining a Positive Attitude Every Day - Lifehack."
    16 Jun. 2022,
    https://www.lifehack.org/articles/communication/11-tips-for-
    maintaining-your-positive-attitude.html.

"80 Examples of a Positive Attitude - Simplicable." 21 Oct. 2021,
    https://simplicable.com/en/positive-attitudes.

"Developing a Positive Attitude - Clarke University."
    https://www.clarke.edu/campus-life/health-
    wellness/counseling/articles-advice/developing-a-positive-
    attitude/.

"Positive thinking: Reduce stress by eliminating negative self-talk
    ...." 03 Feb. 2022, https://www.mayoclinic.org/healthy-
    lifestyle/stress-management/in-depth/positive-thinking/art-
    20043950.

"What Is a Positive Attitude? | HealthyPlace." 04 Jul. 2022,
    https://www.healthyplace.com/self-help/positivity/what-is-a-
    positive-attitude.

"What is Positive Mental Attitude? 9 ways to inculcate it.."
    https://www.proudhr.com/what-is-positive-mental-attitude/.

"21 Ways to Create and Maintain a Positive Attitude."
    https://daringtolivefully.com/positive-attitude.

"The Power of a Positive Attitude - NAHCA | The CNA Association." 20 Mar. 2022, https://www.nahcacna.org/the-power-of-a-positive-attitude/.

"10 Ways To Have a More Positive Attitude at Work | Indeed.com." 12 Dec. 2019, https://www.indeed.com/career-advice/career-development/positive-attitude-at-work.

"5 Ways to Build a Positive Attitude - wikiHow." 17 Mar. 2022, https://www.wikihow.com/Build-a-Positive-Attitude.

"100+ Positive Attitude Quotes for Life - The STRIVE." 18 Nov. 2021, https://thestrive.co/positive-attitude-quotes/.

"Top 7 Benefits Of A Positive Attitude - The STRIVE." 13 Dec. 2021, https://thestrive.co/benefits-of-a-positive-attitude/.

"18 Simple Ways to Keep a Positive Attitude at Work." https://wheniwork.com/blog/18-simple-ways-to-keep-a-positive-attitude-at-work.

"Positive Thinking: Definition, Benefits, and How to Practice." 25 Feb. 2011, https://www.verywellmind.com/what-is-positive-thinking-2794772.

"Positive thinking: Reduce stress by eliminating negative self-talk ...." 03 Feb. 2022, https://www.mayoclinic.org/healthy-lifestyle/stress-management/in-depth/positive-thinking/art-20043950.

"What is positive thinking? 6 ways to use the power of positive thinking." https://www.tonyrobbins.com/positive-thinking/.

"Positive Thinking: What It Is and How to Do It - WebMD." https://www.webmd.com/mental-health/positive-thinking-overview.

"What is Positive Thinking in Psychology? 9 Thought-Provoking Findings." 13 Aug. 2021, https://positivepsychology.com/positive-thinking/.

"Positive Thinking | SkillsYouNeed." https://www.skillsyouneed.com/ps/positive-thinking.html.

"Think Positive: 11 Ways to Boost Positive Thinking." 06 Mar. 2018, https://www.psychologytoday.com/us/blog/click-here-happiness/201803/think-positive-11-ways-boost-positive-thinking.

"Power Of Positive Thinking: 7 Mindful Habits For Positivity." https://thelawofattraction.com/power-of-positive-thinking/.

"The Power of Positive Thinking: 6 Ways to Be Happy All Day Long." 16 Jan. 2019, https://blog.mindvalley.com/the-power-of-positive-thinking/.

"Positive Thinking Quotes (3487 quotes) - Goodreads." https://www.goodreads.com/quotes/tag/positive-thinking.

"What Is Positive Thinking and How to Always Think Positive." https://www.lifehack.org/875426/positive-thinking.

"The Power of Positive Thinking | Benefits of Positive Thinking." 23 Jan. 2016, https://www.jonathanparker.org/mind-power/the-power-of-positive-thinking/.

"What Is Positive Thinking and Why You Need It." https://www.successconsciousness.com/blog/positive-attitude/what-is-positive-thinking/.

"The Power of Positive Thinking | Johns Hopkins Medicine." https://www.hopkinsmedicine.org/health/wellness-and-prevention/the-power-of-positive-thinking.

"Mind Over Matter: The Effects of Positive Thinking - Wright Foundation." 20 Jul. 2017, https://wrightfoundation.org/effects-of-positive-thinking/.

"Benefits of positive thinking: 10 ways to improve life with optimism." 12 Apr. 2022, https://www.betterup.com/blog/positive-thinking-benefits.

"Benefits of positive thinking: 10 ways to improve life with optimism." 12 Apr. 2022, https://www.betterup.com/blog/positive-thinking-benefits.

"Ultimate Positive Thinking Toolkit: 19 Techniques & Exercises." 03 Jan. 2022, https://positivepsychology.com/positive-thinking-exercises/.

"11 Benefits of Positive Thinking and What are They." https://positiveaffirmationscenter.com/benefits-of-positive-thinking/.

"Positive Thinking - How It Impacts Your Life | happiness.com." https://www.happiness.com/positive-thinking/.

"Love Your Enemies" What Jesus Really Meant - Christianity." 04 Oct. 2019, https://www.christianity.com/wiki/christian-life/what-does-it-mean-to-love-your-enemies.html.

"How To Love Your Enemies (6 Practical Tips) - Rethink." 22 Feb. 2021, https://www.rethinknow.org/how-to-love-your-enemies/.

[1] "Love Your Enemies!" What Does It Mean? Can It Be Done?." https://gratefulness.org/resource/love-your-enemies/.

[1] "Love Your Enemies: What It Means And Examples On How To Do So - Pray." 27 Apr. 2021,

https://www.pray.com/articles/love-your-enemies-what-it-means-and-examples-on-how-to-do-so.

[1] "Luke 6:27-36 NIV - Love for Enemies - "But to you who - Bible Gateway." https://www.biblegateway.com/passage/?search=Luke%206:27-36&version=NIV.

[1] "30 Bible verses about Loving Your Enemies - Knowing Jesus." https://bible.knowing-jesus.com/topics/Loving-Your-Enemies.

[1] "A Speech on "The Negative Effects of Selfishness"." https://writolay.com/negative-effects-of-selfishness/.

[1] "4 Ways Selfishness Ruins Your Life - RELEVANT." https://relevantmagazine.com/life5/4-ways-selfishness-ruins-your-life/.

[1] "The Danger of Selfishness." https://www.selfgrowth.com/articles/The_Danger_of_Selfishness.html.

[1] "Selfishness Effects and causes in Human Nature - Actforlibraries.org." http://www.actforlibraries.org/selfishness-effects-and-causes-in-human-nature/.

[1] "Good, Neutral, and Bad Selfishness | Psychology Today." 15 Jan. 2015, https://www.psychologytoday.com/us/blog/cui-bono/201501/good-neutral-and-bad-selfishness.

[1] "Your Selfishness as a Spouse Has a Three-Fold Negative Effect." 15 Jul. 2019, https://www.loveandrespect.com/blog/your-selfishness-as-a-spouse-has-a-three-fold-negative-effect/.

[1] "What are the disadvantages of selfishness? - Quora."
https://www.quora.com/What-are-the-disadvantages-of-
selfishness.